The Alchemy Spoon
Issue 9

The Alchemy Spoon
Issue 9

Editors
Roger Bloor
Vanessa Lampert
Mary Mulholland

Guest Editor
Diana Cant

A poetry magazine with a special interest in 'new phase' poets

Design and production
Clayhanger Press

Typeset in Times New Roman

Poetry Submissions
Our submission window is next open from 1 – 31 May 2023
The theme for the issue is 'Friends'

Please read the submissions guidelines on the final page
Submissions are through the website
www.alchemyspoon.org

Cover Images
Front Cover: *Whitewashing a Rembrandt*, photograph by Gaynor Kane
Back Cover: *Wall in Porto, Portugal*, photograph by Viv Fogel, April 2022

ISSN 2635-0513
ISBN 978-1-7391770-3-4

Contents

Editorial

Audre Lorde writes, 'For there are no new ideas. There are only new ways of making them felt – of examining what those ideas feel like being lived on Sunday morning at 7a.m., after brunch, during wild love, making war, giving birth, mourning our dead – while we suffer the old longings, battle the old warnings and fears of being silent and impotent and alone; while we taste new possibilities and strengths.'[1]

It is an enormous privilege and a pleasure to be the guest editor of this graffiti-themed issue of *The Alchemy Spoon*. The theme, perhaps unsurprisingly, drew a high number of artwork submissions which really warranted showcasing, so we have decided to feature some of these images, not only on the covers, but inside the magazine as well. We think they make a lively addition to some stunning poems.

Lorde says that our drive to communicate ideas to others often propels us towards experimenting with new ways of doing this. But there is a timelessness to graffiti, be it imprecations on a Pompeii wall or masked gunmen in Belfast, that can be both particular and universal. Graffiti – depending on where you look and whom you trust – is broadly defined as having three main features. It is a visual form of communication that is both public, and illegal. Its public visibility means it is often associated with protest, both political and personal. Its illegality (which, arguably, differentiates it from street art) can arouse fairly irritated responses – a cursory trawl of the internet reveals some rather ill-tempered local council postings!

We hope that what we've offered you here doesn't arouse the same degree of ire. The poets in this issue have responded to the theme in a variety of creative ways: there are poems that address the overtly political, and poems whose canvas is smaller scale and domestic. There are poems that focus on the inherent, haunting mystery in the messaging, and others that are anchored in childhood, or in love. There are those that move away from the wall as backdrop and use the skin or the body, while some are humorous, or written just for the sheer joy of it. Perhaps we shouldn't be surprised that all human life is here, and that vandalism and art can go hand in hand. 'Poetry (and graffiti) is taking the arguments onto the

---

[1] Audre Lorde, Poetry is Not a Luxury, 1977, *Strong Words,* ed *Herbert and Hollis* (Bloodaxe Books, 2000)

streets, trying to engage and persuade ordinary people of its worth and meaning', to slightly misquote Simon Armitage. [2]

This issue carries, rather appropriately, a feeling of accessibility and immediacy. Mary Mulholland's enlightening and enlivening interview with Ian McMillan is full of wise and straightforward reflection, covering a vast territory, but always returning to Yorkshire. Di Slaney, editor and publisher of Candlestick Press, writes about her life as poet, publisher and livestock-sanctuary provider. Helen Mort is our featured poet and reads from her Forward Prize shortlisted collection, *The Illustrated Woman*, where her remarkable poems live on the skin, and from her 2019 collaboration with Aaron Meskin, *Opposite: Poems, Philosophy and Coffee*. All this work resonates with our theme, with lived life-experience vibrating at its heart.

There are also reviews from Julian Bishop, SK Grout, Sue Wallace-Shaddad, Mary Mulholland and Tamsin Hopkins, suggesting yet more poetic explorations. But the last words of this editorial should go to Banksy:

'Art should comfort the disturbed and disturb the comfortable…speak softly, but carry a big can of paint.' [3]

Diana Cant

---

[2] Simon Armitage, Re-Writing the Good Book, *Strong Words,* ed *Herbert and Hollis* (Bloodaxe Books, 2000)
[3] https://www.goodreads.com/author/quotes/28811.Banksy

Instinct

Give us spit, mixed
with clay, a stub of pencil
lead, a tin of paint,
a purple lipstick, or
a rusty knife.
Provide a cave wall,
a tree trunk, a school desk,
a billboard, a park
bench, a toilet cubicle,
and we will come –
eager to leave our mark,
to reach out to those
who will walk after us,
to set our words in line
with those who walked before.
This is the nub of who we are.
It is what being human is –
the social consequence of ink,
the act of carving out our shape,
the frail democracy of art.

Rachel Carney

Instructions for Tagging

LEMON DEMON. SOOP DOG. KEK
First practise your tag. Don't use
your real name for obvious reasons.
Initials will do or a symbol,
BOYO. HGA. LAYER
something distinctive, something
that shows up, that other taggers
will respect. When you're confident
you can reproduce it over and over,
take your can of spray paint
and go looking for the perfect spot.
PIRRA. BAXER. CWEL
Walls are good, anything from
a tunnel to a ginnel, but play safe,
work in dark places, railway sidings,
alleyways, subways and tube trains,
passages and back lanes and parking lots,
old phone boxes and building sites,
MAK. BAZ. OMAR. CREEM
anywhere away from people and CCTV
and barking dogs and squad cars.
The trick is to be quick,
leave your mark, walk away,
whistling, head down, hood up,
the can in your inside pocket.
TOAD. BIZ. JUNO
I'm here. I exist. This is mine.

Carole Bromley

Leaving your mark

May things go happily for Anicia
Beware, Timinia: thieves!
Let the bears devour me
scrawled on walls in Herculaneum

Pacatus stayed here in Pompeii with his friends.
We came, we came here desiring,
much more do we desire to go
among the ruins of Pompeii

Scratched on the bottom corner
of a panel of York Minster glass
Thomas Clarke, plumber and glazier,
July 4th, 1794, aged 15

Even in the Ice Age they were at it
painting on cave walls
with fruit juice, minerals, animal blood
before writing was invented

I, too, in the sixties, gouged out
with a compass point in a desk lid
City for the cup!
scratched CD=TR on my ruler

yet, teaching, I told a boy off
for not copying my notes off the board,
instead scrawling on his jotter
Catherine, Catherine, Catherine

Carole Bromley

Witch's Castle

The excitement grew as we left
the interstate and slipped
onto the Beltway, almost home.
The sky was clear, the sun had set.
The building would be beautiful that night,
for sure.

They'd placed it where
it would suddenly appear as if by magic,
as if rising from the roadway
and not beside it. Looking bigger than
it really was, like the God they built it for.

Lit by floodlights, but looking more
like something glowing from within,
the tombstone-colored marble
forming towers, walls and
spires in imitation of the Gothic,
but looking more like an edifice
from Oz, in Deco. A wizard's or a witch's castle.
Either one, but not the church it thought it was.

Curving toward it, we saw Gabriel
blowing silently as we sucked our
breath in, hoping it hadn't been
erased again (as if boring squares
of beige atop each letter were really an
erasure), and, thank God, there it was.

Scrawled upon the rusted metal
overpass that acted as marquee
for the building right beyond,
just two words, the triumph
of one wag over a monolith of faith
spelled out in spray paint:
'Surrender Dorothy!'

Donald Sellitti

Fountain Penning

Blotting my rough work book with I love yous
on the first date wasn't really a good idea. KWs got
fountain-penned everywhere: the white birch tree

bark behind the bike sheds, a Helix rubber marked
up like vellum codex, a closed book's edge that hadn't
rejected the flat-pressed kiss of ink, and eventually

my own skin too, where it didn't show. And for who?
Not Kim Wilde, Kirsty Wark, Kanye yet, but just
those letters welling up Quinky, in blue-black graffiti.

    and those one thousand
four hundred and forty-five souls listed
        on peoplebyinitials.com so far

where the wild things are as well as
    all before them
    from Good King Wenceslas to

    Kurt Weill
    to Kenneth Williams and
the many Wolffs reminding me

    I loved you then
even the bad linked ones I never got to know
    written out in notes above/below

Mark Saunders

Carving Out a Career

He smiles at the long frill of wood as he trims
yet another pencil, gently testing each tip
on the palm of a hand.

He would like to go on sharpening like this
until the bell goes. It is an ideal lunchtime
in his opinion.

But another pupil waits to use the sharpener
so he drifts to a desk, sits, carves rapid letters
with his pencil into wood.

He covers them with a hand as I approach:
Please don't do that, it's damaging the desk.
I give him paper instead.

He returns to the sharpener, smiles at the long
frill of wood as he trims, gently testing each tip
on the palm of a hand.

Dear Sirs, he has carved. *Yours is my dream job.*
I know I am not like other applicants. But I am...
I have cut across his dream.

Claudia Court

On learning to swear

I didn't know *shit* was bad until my joke
made dad disappointed, not angry.

The milkman was a *wally*. Grandpa once
said damn when he hammered his thumb,

but if mum stubbed a toe it was *heck* or *blow*,
or, for some reason, bush (no hint of a pun).

Families like ours didn't swear or shout.
We s*ugared, blimeyed, flipped* and buttoned

our lips until middle age. But, oh,
the *nob-ends* and *wankers* I curse now!

How they *bugger things up* for the rest of us
with their *bloody stupid ideas*. It's all *bollocks*!

The words feel *fucking fantastic*, all hard edges
and squat vowels, like the kids we weren't allowed

to play with, circling the estate on their bikes,
spitting graffiti at pebble-dashed bungalows.

Alison Binney

Urban Melodies

Sunday treats are trips to the toy shop in Derry.
Bungalow kids, we love its sweeping staircase,
the deep pile carpet spongy as a waterlogged bog.

We mull over Sindy dolls, edgy in our knee-high
socks and Mary Janes. There's too much stuff
and not enough time. Graffitied shutters

on the way say *Brits Out* and *Tiocfaidh ár Lá*.
A spray paint can rolls around in the wind,
clanks an urban melody.

It's all abandoned bags, bomb scares, Mum
tearing at a hangnail and the looming threat
of being pulled from the shop in panic.

I shuffle to the window, watch baby-faced lads
patrol Shipquay Street's steep incline with rifles
and soft chin contours yet to meet a razor's glide.

Their bovver boots glossy as Tate & Lyle's treacle,
catch slivers of streetlight and above us that other world,
where instead of counting pavement cracks

on the way back to the car, I keep my head up, forever
alert to atmospheric changes, my head in the clouds
decoding the splendour of Canis Major, Sirius and The Plough.

Lorraine Carey

Blast Radius. Burj Hammud

On the steel door of an old garment factory
a local Banksy has spray painted a child
dragging her pram full of rocket grenades.
Inside, stray cats scatter across rusty hangers.
The reek is cut with secret fires and weed.
Peace signs weep on a wall jazzed with hate.
Faded cigarette ads depict ancient visitors
from Beirut's Golden Age of Discotheque.
FRESH. CALM. MILD. ONLY KOOLS.
Four white people in white on a white yacht
ghost thin white pleasures for the departed.
COME TO WHERE THE FLAVOUR IS.
A Marlboro man with Saddam mustache
sits on a horse with his eyes burned out.
A postcard Madonna smiles with tiny Jesus
who pulls aside her hijab as if to share a joke
here in the city that still smokes with faith.
Down the hallway, an art deco chandelier
begins to glimmer like an electric dandelion.
Outside, a cheer. The generators are back on.

Mark Fiddes

Valley of the pilgrims

Scoured by Sinai wind and sun, Armenians
rest in the sandstone shade of Wadi Haggag,
carving their new alphabet into stone.

Remember sinful Yakuv / Remember Kaspar /
I, Pawlos wrote this inscription in the year 301/
He who reads it let you remember me

One thousand miles from home, they scratch
the granite cliffs of Wadi Mukatab, Valley of Inscriptions,
while their guides go to fetch desert water.

Lord have mercy on the camel and the guide / Lord
have mercy on Eliab / Anto / Eram / Simeon / Elisa / Adrint
Ode / Cucut / T'at'anoys / Vasak the monk / Ners

They carve cross after cross after Armenian cross.
I made this khatchkar in the year 420 / Unworthy /Disobedient/
Babgen / T'ouma / Abraham / Anania / Natan / Stepanos /

I have seen Jerusalem / I have circumambulated Moses /
I visited St Catherine in the year of the Armenians 912 /
Martiros / Astuacatur / Bagrat / Krikor / remain here

Pilgrim paleography of boredom / fear / faith
scratched on the north and east of the rocks in noon heat
with sweating fingers, slipping knives, streaming eyes.

Sarah Mnatzaganian

Kharkiv Words

they wouldn't let me out
to cut the grass
says Anna
or prune the bushes
because that's where
they hid their snipers

what they did not destroy
they stole
they took forks and spoons
and then shoes
from the pensioners feet
in Kharkiv

and on these walls graffiti
in Russian

the game is over
and
sorry

Ian Ledward

Written On the Skin

In July, '*I love sex*' appeared overnight,
in a jagged script on the wall opposite your office.

The man you loved back then
got your name inked on his arm the same summer.

Graffiti on a condemned building, he joked
when he revealed the lettering.

His tattoo was still bleeding when he tore off the plastic.
The letters were in an uneven font, as if sprayed on stone.

It was hot at work that year.
Your boss told you that in those flimsy tops
you made the dial spin on his pacemaker.

The lads on the factory floor made comments too
but you never seemed to have time to complain

with life hurtling forward as fast as the machines
which poured out sticky words 24/7

But two things happen come autumn –
the printing factory closes and the machines stop,
and he leaves you after another row.

A year later, you get the letter inviting you to his funeral.
As you read it the words bleed.

And you imagine your name sinking under the earth,
those letters breaking down to nothing,

like the printing company demolished for a new road,
and the graffitied wall, smashed down into rubble.

Anna Saunders

22

23

A rescue

As I undress you, they catch my eye
two yellowed finger-marks
a fading signature, stark
on your rounded thigh.

a scarlet circle, crusting yellow
decorates your chest
I order photographs and tests
dreading what must follow

White lumpy shadows on a screen:
telltale callus on healing ribs.
You cry, small whining sobs
in your mother's arms as I explain.

We start with outrage and denials
then, confronted with the evidence
she lapses into sullen silence
as nurses take her child.

There are no good choices for you,
chancing the kindness of strangers
or hoping you survive home's danger:
finding the least bad rescue

Rob Primhak

Post-mastectomy celebration

Their chests, walls of ivy: thorned roses
        reaching from pit to solar plexus. A flutter
of bird wings, a butterfly's thorax, a mermaid's
        modest shell. Wire, barbed with daisies
        reclaims this space, these territories.

Millie Light

The Vegetarian, Plastic Ono Band Fan

I forget on which motorway bridge it was applied.
I recall it was neat, white, writing.
I don't know how it got close to the underside.
I imagine a trusted mate holding on tight to thighs.

Sue Spiers

Gianna e Fede

On the Piazza Cavour in Viareggio,
in a crude, spray-painted scrawl,
the names *Gianna e Fede*,
bookmarked by large blue hearts.

It's nice to know that teenage love
is still publicly demonstrative –
that in any language the urge to tell
the world is undiminished.

Where are they now, *Gianna e Fede*?
Did one of them move away
to Milano, leaving the other
to work the beach clubs, alone?

Or are they like Tommy and Gina
in *Livin' on A Prayer* – holding on
to what they've got, which is each other?
Sometimes I think of them like that.

Georgia Hilton

Ben, please phone Dad

        is written in red paint
on two columns of the roundabout
off the city bypass. It hasn't faded
over the years.

        Who crossed the busy road
with a can of spray paint and a stencil?
Why was Ben contacted by graffiti
and did he ever make that call?

        I drive past every week
and think about Ben and his Dad.
It gnaws at my heart what was said
or what was never said.

        How many other Bens
have rung their Dads since then
and been greeted with gruff joy
at the sound of their voice?

Rebecca Gethin

concrete confession

I had to tell you I loved you
just before we walked down the steps
to the graffiti subway under the A4,
not because I was overcome by my feelings,
but frankly because that was the moment
where the emotional labour of not telling you
became simply too exhausting and –
to be completely honest – also kind of boring,
and that is such an unromantic reason
that perhaps even you could approve of it.

Deborah Finding

SHOCKER

at the end of my street
a vacant lot
bustling with poppies
blooming early!
seasonal defiance!
I drop by each day
seeing
on the sidewall of the neighbouring house
only curtains of ivy   copperplated
but today
floating in bubble letters
a graffito
l   o   v   e
the window of its 'e'
open to gritted teeth
so nobody dare
wash it off

Kit Ingram

Juliet's House, Verona

Above a courtyard, through a dark archway,
Juliet's balcony shines as though holy,
while stone walls below show a different story:
how love can lead to a pox of graffiti.

What's in a name? Or two names and a date?
They multiplied on her house like a plague
in black and blue ink, or red and white paint,
though a sign says: *Do not smear and deface.*

There were star-cross'd lovers. Heart-shaped lovers.
Lumps of gum used to stick lovers' letters.
Covered up lovers. Names scrawled on plasters.
Even a couple of lovers' French letters.

And now Verona is known as the city
of tragic love and forbidden graffiti.

Thea Smiley

road trip palimpsest

we're heading to Chafiras on the Los Abrigos road
hire car's a manual   bigger than I'm used to   traffic's heavy
plus there's left-hand drive to deal with here *stop/wait/go*
                              sun's hot on my left cheek   my neck
the arm resting like a boy cruiser's
                              on the open window *stop/wait/give way/go*
your local knowledge is better than mine but
            you're struggling to help me *wait/look*
                                    the road markings are confusing *look*
                  flaky patches of old white paint still visible
beneath the new
                        like a schoolchild's maths diagram subject to
                        repeated rubbings-out *look*
sometimes the old and new markings are
                        completely at variance *look/look*
arrows left becoming arrows right
                        chevrons and hatches so inexpertly
covered over they still seem to carry some of their
                                    original weight
a half-obscured zebra unsure whether or not it's safe to cross
a S T P missing one
                        crucial letter

Sarah Hemings

The Effect of Temperature and Salinity

_It'^s unread]able - code-fray/ed pages
a@nd ~wa#t{er st+aining
wo]rds ^as numb£er stri_ng~s
afte+r Lan''*gstone{ Ha:rbour flowe#d in/

odd$ charac/ters sten_cil-spraye@d
<the margi=]n with o///ysterc:atchers
and d)u1nlins #p#rising open
sa+n\d-damaged fl"oppy£ -di]sk[s

+A bi"valve\/ gets ;re-dr~awn
pix!el by pi%xel - pea>rl.y
}and im*pre¬ssionisti$c abo<v>^e
,apo\stroph~es fo4r po+sses+sio/n er¬rors

Ro[ckpoo%ls hol)d fi~eld"wor}k
f4or s>ex ide/ntif£icati!on- - he+r biol^ogy
c|ourse&wo*rk) uno#pen.abl!e
{the= b%ody te\xt cau'g$ht}_up~

Mark Saunders

Writ in water

In a park in China
a tall elegant old man

and a small girl in pink
are writing characters

on the paving stones,
with water. They come

every day. Their brushes,
moving in tandem, are fed

by tanks they wear around
their waists. The old man

also wears, swinging loose,
a kitsch medallion of Mao.

Their strokes are like
dancing, Tai Chi. As soon

as each ideogram appears
the thirsty sun sucks it up

and it is gone. And what I
write, will it last more

than a watery moment?
I pick up my brush, start.

Veronica Zundel

Retirement

is like renovating
the house you've lived in
all your life

gutting it to the outside walls
or adding a coat of paint
at pace no youth could bear

one wall or closet
door or drawer
at a time

listening with new attention
to the creaking floor
between bed and bath

rocking the empty
porch swing
with rusted chains

an arthritic finger
tracing the heart
with initials
in the attic joist

the marks with names
on the pantry wall

wrecking ball still
in a gallery of glaze

Michael Lyle

Graffito

Your house, last night,
large moon, street lamps,
me with a paint brush.
I was going to write:
LOVE ME, ONLY ME
in lime green letters,
Times New Roman.
But Anon beat me to it.
I've added my signature.

Rod Whitworth

A New Daub

Condemnation never lacks language. – John Montague

Tired, I came home from work one day to discover
someone had painted, in the simple calligraphy of anger,
a word on the brick wall between the door to my flat
and my new next door neighbour's kitchen window:
WHORE
Clearly her ex was not happy and neither were we;
we both set-to with solvent and scrubbing brushes.
                    WHORE
at first simply became a little blurry. Exhausted
we took a break, hoping time 'the great healer'
would eventually obliterate the words. Next day
we had another go. We scrubbed and scrubbed
                         WHORE
eventually took on a ghostly pallor, as if our collective
exorcism was gradually forcing it to retreat into the brick.
But we still had to live with a faint reprimand. Perhaps
the weather would finish it off. For weeks traces of
                        WHORE
lingered as a spectral presence but after we sanded down
the wall the word lost its bite until it discreetly faded away.

Colin Pink

When a thirteen year old loses her mother

she wants to write her pain on everything.
We were good girls, swots,
sticklers for rules and high grades.

So Sophie's shock shift
into loud expletives and trowelled-on
make-up was hard to take.

Harder still were the nightly forays
with older boys I was forbidden from seeing.

She seemed to think they held the key
to the place where love went.

These lucky guys used their keys–
got to *unlock* her regularly.

She began to write her hate on every available surface.
Walls got it, toilet doors got it.

Her mistake was scrawling it
on the maths book of a boy

who punched teachers
and smoked crack and could not spell–
Fuck me. I love dirty pricks.

Michelle Diaz

Sticky Little Crustaceans / Figurehead

Her dad pushed her to take the job
spend that summer down at the boat yard
safely stowed, while teenage boys sunbathed
with ice in the hollow of their breast bones
like a talisman against the heat,

she stripped barnacles and coral-ish growths
from triple-layered mahogany hulls,
the *Ellie Marie*, *One of My Girls*, *Our Legacy*,
each one lifted from the water like a carcass
to undergo the stainless steel of the scraper,

but on every boat, she carved a naked girl
with a putty knife just below the waterline,
she liked to imagine them out at sea
two spared barnacles proud as nipples
giving forth: a pair of feathery tongues.

Emma Ormond

Lundy Island, Bristol Channel

1.

Stubborn as the head of an old flat nail
stood proud of the grain, a danger to slipping

fingers making glib passage over dry
parallels to a channel swell, never

suspecting the force, the sheer stop-and-slice
in an oblong block of granite that is

three miles long and old as the sea

2.

Words like cauldron, scale, and fulmar flit past
as spit in the wind – here, where air havers

(those slow huff instants, clung to the highest
frozeframe toppling blocks) then is lost at sea.

All of us, migrants – birds, even the scribed graffiti
on neolithic graves, christian headstones –

all passing through, all time-ground, ash and dust.

3.

Here's the hut where we friends, migratory,
stop quiet as wind's quick lull, auscultate

a nearer past; bold piracy, slavers' gold.
Bristol-bound ships passed right by here, watched

by bright puffins, shedding spoiled cargoes which
won't melt in time as mere stone – still stand hard,

proud, sharp as any of the dead we build upon.

Dickon Bevington

Spells for Blackening the Page

1
Haunt me, silverfish,
dead of night
by this ash-feathered
fireside;
with old ghosts
shivering the window,
haunt me
by the words I write.

2
Haunt me, ysbryd,
in the Churchyard
of Brecon Cathedral,
in a Caerphilly lane,
or holed up
in your native mountains
of Crimea,
ghost slug, haunt me.

3
Haunt me, albino whale
pursued by Ahab,
haunt me,
Ishmael's fear of pale;
through the closing
prospect
of nothingness,
haunt me, Melville.

Patrick Deeley

Going Camping

when shit attains a value, the poor man
will be born without an arsehole

A country inn among the fells –
flock wallpaper and horse brasses,
the flattened carpet with a swirling pattern.
We take our ale swiftly – town boys
getting messed up in somewhat of a rush.

We don't write home – there's nothing
to say and no one really wishes
we were there. Used beer is offloaded
in an outdoor urinal, this wisdom on the wall
it has not been possible to forget.

Oliver Comins

Leaving Gracia

Tourists Fuck Off. Four bloody stripes.
The flag is daubed on every wall.
The Catalans are tough. G says
'No soc tourist, jo soc artist.'
I'm just the artist's wife. I drift.
My Catalan is bad, I know.
I go to local thrift shops, buy
the local clothes and food. They scowl
and shrug. I keep my head down low.
The local wine is cheap enough.

The waitress at our favourite bar
keeps selling us her most expensive
gin and whisky. Throws in shots.
Changes the tunes when we walk in.
I drink too much, laugh, sing along.
Jo soc tourista, si, es clar.
Comfortably numbed, we pay and pay,
Buying belief that we belong.
Tourists fuck off. Tourists go home.
This town has artists of its own.

Jane Hughes

The genetics of concrete

On the streets at night,
men walk with their names in their pockets,
under bridges, on rooftops, in back alleys;
they bomb the walls their fathers built.

It's taken decades
to squeeze men into spray paint cans:
their blood makes 94 BLACK,
their tears make SILVER SATISFACTION.

A lineage of nightwalkers,
fingers on triggers,
crouching in trenches,
they rattle the same bones,

an aerosol prayer -
they ask the chemicals to burn holes
through their lungs, so that one day,
their sons and daughters might breathe

through concrete
into a new city, moulded by softer hands,
into an old city, where, on the streets at night
they would recall their mothers

passing beneath these same bridges,
clutching handbags like funeral flowers,
eyes darting between the shadows
of broken spines

wondering
whose blood, whose tears, whose sons would paint the walls tonight;
their index fingers ready
on the pepper spray in their pockets.

Robyn Perros

Carmine, the bespoke tailor, Brooklyn
for Mona Panitz

A petite man, Carmine
was an aproned dresser
when he sewed.

Each stitch taped
by a martinet,
his suits outlined his life.

His personal *accoutrements*
a dainty ensemble
of cufflinks, tie clip and collar pin.

His opinions, pronouncements:
despising Mussolini,
detesting Fascism,

the Pope a non-entity,
anyone south of Rome suspect.
Each morning hatless

he made his way
to the subway newsstand
to be handed his *New York Times*.

His work bespoke, he held his wife's
cooking to the same standards. When her
meatballs and sauce

did not measure up, he hurled the pot
against the dining room wall,
an eruption not unlike Mount Vesuvius

splattering molten red sauce
that oozed down the plasterboard,
flooded the hardwood floor,

pooling round islands
of floored meatballs,
invoking his name.

Roger Camp

48

The Sitting

Line is long. Lean in, if you would. Four, eight, thirteen that's tragic. Where's wood to touch? Maybe one or two of you could fall out. And you madam or sir, sorry can't see, arch away from the chap on your left. Great! Goblet and food front and centre, so obvious supper. Perhaps an upset salt cellar. Blimey, you all look like it's the last time together. Say leaven bread … no one has died, right?

Did I hear talk of travelling to Gaul? I'm off there once … hallelujah, colourful reactions, was there something shocking? Snap in my head. Moment frozen. Don't fret, secrets safe, this fresco will be an enigma, assuming it's even seen. Also, remember I'm one of many graffiti artists, likely to be forgotten quickly.

Jill Vance

The Artist

You thought I wouldn't guess
where you went those nights
teenager, hooded like a monk
cans of paint clinking
like secret treasure
in an old school backpack.

Sometimes I'd spot your skilful tag
bright, blooming in the desert
of concrete and steel
on a dull grey shutter or
derelict wall that seemed to be
crying out for colour

And I know I really ought
to have disapproved
imposed some sort of curfew
or at least said something
but all I could think to say was -
Work fast. Don't get caught.

Eileen Farrelly

50

WOT FOR? WHY NOT?

December, 3 o'clock.
Not the best time for a journey,
no camels, only the old blue car.
The engine stammers,
chokes and stops. 'Kiss the car, boys.'
They kiss her and she starts. A shout of triumph from the back.

East London, Bow, the other side of the city.
It's getting dark, dusk
and cold allying bitterly in the empty park.
Orange streetlights give a spectral glow.
We crunch across frosted grass,
the boys collide and rebound, shout to hear their voices
echo in the cold thin air,
the inside-out house ahead of us, bare ground on either side,
no cosy terrace nursing it.

We stand quiet,
see the pale concrete slab
see the stairs and windows jut
into air; the light switches
reversed; graffiti,
WOT FOR? WHY NOT?
black against the walls.

Deb Catesby

*Rachel Whiteread's public sculpture, 'House', was demolished on
11th January 1994*

52

A Personal View

Di Slaney considers a very particular intersection of the worlds of poetry and animal welfare

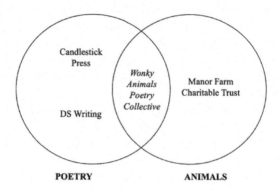

So there it is: my life in a Venn diagram. Any questions? Of course you have questions! It looks like a very odd assembly of things that don't really go together, doesn't it? Some days it feels like that, and then other days there's something magical in the air that brings all the disparate clucking, baaing, bleating and stomping aspects of my work and personal life together into a strange but satisfying chaos.

Depending on how you know me, if you know me, I'm either the woman with all the animals in a very old farmhouse on the edge of Sherwood Forest, or the publisher and editor of Candlestick Press, or the poet who writes about history, sex and goats, or one of the passionate members of the Wonky Animal Poetry Collective. You might have the misfortune to know me for all of these things, in which case I can only apologise for bombarding you with information from every angle on social media.

I didn't set out to live a complicated life. In 2010 I was starting to write poems again after a 20-year hiatus and completing the MA in Creative Writing at Nottingham Trent University. An opportunity arose to see if poetry could become commercially successful when I joined Candlestick Press as co-owner, later becoming sole owner and editor of the press. Juggling writing my own poems with the production of mini-anthologies of the work of other poets has been tricky – anyone who works in poetry publishing and is also a poet will tell you that it can be hard to hear your own voice when there are so many other brilliant voices filling your eyes, ears and mind.

At Candlestick we believe that poetry is for everyone, so each of our pamphlets has a theme that we're confident lots of people will love – everything from bees to baking, home to happiness and sheds to sheep. The idea is that we can bring people to poetry by introducing them to a range of poets writing about their enthusiasms – acting as a signpost to the poets' other work and a springboard into the wider world of poetry beyond that particular pamphlet. It's an important distinction, as we're largely publishing for 'civilians' (non-poets!) but poets also buy our work for themselves and their civilian friends and family, thereby widening the poetry circle we all love and are invested in.

Candlestick pamphlets are gift products, complete with envelopes and a bookmark for writing a personal message from gifter to giftee. I'm evangelical about the work that we do in broadening the reach of poetry in this way, and I read every customer comment and track every customer order. We're stocked by chain and independent bookshops, galleries, and gift shops across the UK and into Ireland. You'll find us in some unexpected places: we also count garden centres, wool shops, bakeries, cafés, and hairdressers amongst our stockists, along with some prestigious names like the British Museum and the Eden Project. We've recently started exporting to Australia and I'm really excited about the potential of this new market.

But what about the animals? Where did they come from and how do they fit in? In 2011 my husband and I had the opportunity to buy the field next to our 400-year-old farmhouse, re-attaching land back to the farm on the historic Danish defensive mound in the centre of our village. My husband thought that he was protecting our property from further development whereas I had another idea in mind – to bring life back to the old farm, but in a non-commercial way. Starting with four hens in the garden, we took on some disabled and elderly livestock who needed extra care at the end of their lives and then the numbers started to creep up, as did the variety of species. Donkeys, ponies, pigs, goats, sheep, ducks, chickens, geese, quail – all in need of a home for life and special care.

We gained registered charity status as Manor Farm Charitable Trust in 2017 and now have over 180 animals on site. We offer lifelong sanctuary for livestock in need. There's a small employed team helping us, along with dedicated volunteers who love the animals as much as we do. It's a whole heap of work and worry, of course – animals with special needs demand more time and medication, which means more cost, which means more fundraising. And this is where the intersection in the Venn diagram comes in…

A discussion with the marvellous Clare Shaw towards the end of 2022 about the poetry of animals rapidly led to an explosion of ideas about how the vulnerabilities of humans and animals overlap and can generate great poetry. Our little group expanded to include more marvellous human beings with Anna Barker, Kathryn Bevis, Jane Burn and Tania Hershman kicking the project up to a whole new level. The Wonky Animals Poetry Collective was born! We're all poets who engage with life from an animal perspective – and in doing so, we generate a deeper humanity towards creatures, each other, and our own wonky selves. Very generously, the Wonky Poets donate their time to raise money to support the wonky animals at the sanctuary by running readings, workshops, and events. The response so far has been amazing – generous audiences and a full involvement with the spirit of the initiative. I'm so grateful and very moved by this support, as well as the privilege of hearing some fantastic poems by brilliant writers. Do come join us at one of our events – we all have a little wonky in us that deserves to be explored!

My own wonkiness and the lives of the animals have become increasingly intertwined in both my life and my writing, with a brain tumour diagnosis in 2019 turning my world upside down for a while. The animals were a great comfort in that difficult early time of coming to terms with new limitations and a different way of seeing the world. At some point most of us will have a health upset that will change the way we view ourselves – with luck, we get a chance to do something positive with that altered perspective. Animals don't worry about what they've lost – they live in the moment, making the best of every opportunity to not only survive but thrive. At the sanctuary we've had the saddest and most unhopeful creatures become the most joyful, finding new ways to get around if they're immobilised or a different way of eating if they're physically challenged to eat normally. They're an inspiration and a wonder.

I live an imperfect, messy, demanding life overflowing with poems, poets, pamphlets, and perfectly-imperfect creatures. How lucky am I?

Di Slaney

Candlestick Press www.candlestickpress.co.uk / Twitter: @poetrycandle / Instagram: @candlestickpress.
Manor Farm Charitable Trust www.manorfarmcharitabletrust.org with current news on the charity's Facebook page.

Wonky Animals Poetry Collective is a private group on Facebook with new members very welcome – see Eventbrite for latest events.

Works by Di Slaney
Dad's Slideshow (Stonewood Press, 2015)
Reward for Winter (Valley Press, 2016)
Herd Queen (Valley Press, 2020)

The Interview

Ian McMillan is a household name, renowned for his warm humour presenting the TS Eliot readings and the Friday evening arts programme *The Verb* on BBC Radio 3. Poet, performer, playwright, presenter, Ian answers twenty questions put to him by **Mary Mulholland**

MM: Ian, thank you for agreeing to this interview. You have such a prodigious career and immense output it's hard to know where to begin. Let's start with: what were your literary origins? Were there books at home? Had there been writers in the family before you?

IMcM: I always put my literary origins down to three things: my dad's Great Aunt Bella Howatson was a Victorian poet who used to write my dad rhyming letters; her work was published in anthologies and although it was typical of the verse of the time, she was always seen as an important figure, and it was always implicitly and explicitly understood that poetry was important, and that poets were interesting people.

My mam and dad met as pen pals in the second world war. He was in the Navy, and she was in the WAAFs, and there was a scheme at that time where single service-people could write to each other. It's a beautiful story; they only met a few times before they got married and then they got married on a 48-hour pass because it was the war and who knew what the future would hold. I always think that writing is important to me because they met through writing.

Thirdly, I always cite the West Riding of Yorkshire and the visionary genius Sir Alec Clegg, the Chief Education Officer, who said that all children were creative. So, our little school in a pit village was like an arts centre: we sang, we danced, we drew, we painted, and we wrote endless poems, so that for me writing poems became as natural as breathing. One day I'll make a radio documentary about Alec Clegg!

MM: I read you wanted to be a writer all through your schooldays, 'but no one from Yorkshire was making it in the arts,' though there was Ted Hughes. Was he a shining light? Was there a particular teacher?

IMcM: Because of those three influences, I wanted to be a writer; writing was seen as an important thing that somehow would change the world. I remember reading John Steinbeck after seeing *The Grapes of Wrath* on Sunday afternoon TV, and I followed the story of Alexander Solzhenitsyn escaping from Soviet Russia and winning the Nobel Prize. I was endlessly encouraged by my parents and by one teacher at secondary school in particular, Mr Brown, who told me that I could be a poet. I think that's why I always endlessly encourage people who want to be writers.

MM: 1977/78 seems to have been quite a turning point. You'd have been about 22, 23? Can you say something about this? For example, from 'Christmas morning 1978' (from *Batteries not included*): 'I have been given/ the small black balaclava of language', and in another poem, about summer 1977, you went to America for two weeks which 'affected me profoundly'...

IMcM: I haven't really thought much about 1977/78 except that they were an exciting time for me because I'd had my road trip to America on a Greyhound Bus. I'd just left North Staffs Poly and got a job on a building site, I was saving up to get married, I was reading my poems in folk clubs, I was getting work published in magazines; the world felt full of promise.

MM: Who were your poetry influences? There's a line in 'Lumb Bank, 1978' : 'something starts here'. Were those tutors particularly influential, or did you do courses and have mentoring?

IMcM: My two big influences were Dylan Thomas and Ted Hughes; they were almost too influential, and they nearly swamped me. They were both in an anthology we read at school called *Nine Modern Poets*; I loved the word-drunkenness of Thomas, and I loved the fact that Hughes was a Yorkshireman who didn't live that far from me. Their work cast a shadow over mine for years, though.

I went to Lumb Bank a few times when I was first starting out: the first course would have been in 1976 where the tutors were Alan Brownjohn and Pete Morgan. Pete, in particular, was a huge influence on me, partly because he made his living as a freelance poet in lots of ways: gigs, schools, writing, TV and Radio, bits of commercial writing, and that's a route I've followed. The guest reader on that course was the now sadly neglected poet Harold Massingham, who was an almost exact contemporary of Ted Hughes at Mexborough Grammar School. On the Charles Sisson course he was co-tutor with Fleur Adcock, and David Wright was the guest reader; he was remarkable, a survivor of an older generation of poets. He was deaf, and his wife Pippa read his poems for him. He and Charles Sisson encouraged me to send poems to Carcanet Press, who became one of my publishers.

MM: In the early 1980s you stopped working in a factory because of a bursary from Yorkshire Arts. I wonder how that came about?

IMcM: I was getting quite a lot of work doing gigs and workshops and found that the regular job (I'd left the building site and was working in a tennis ball factory) was getting in the way. At the time (1983) Yorkshire Arts were giving out grants of up to £1000 if you gave your job up. It's a lot of money now but it was a huge amount then. I applied for it, and they gave me £800 which isn't much less but felt like a lot less. Luckily my wife (who was working as a teacher) and my parents were supportive and told me to give up my job. So I did. And here I am!

MM: Do you workshop your own poetry with groups? I read you prefer to write with people and life happening all around you.

IMcM: I'm not a member of a workshop so I just bang away at my work on my own. I do like to work downstairs on the dining table rather than in a study because, yes, I do like the swirl of life around me. It helps me to think.

MM: Can you share your thoughts on performance vs page poetry? In one book you wrote 'these poems are to be read aloud.'

IMcM: One of my problems is that I'm not a great critic, so I see performance and page poetry as part of the same broad, wide church. I try not to exclude anybody, any style, any genre, any form. Having said that, I always test out my poems on the ear, but that's because I've always been a performer and a listener.

MM: I know you run workshops yourself, so I wonder what your opinion is of the modern trend for workshops, doing MA/ PhD, taking a Mentor? And the post-pandemic explosion of poetry?

IMcM: I love them; the more the better. I've always (because of my West Riding Schooling) been of the opinion that everyone is creative and that we can all be poets, we can all improve our skills. The problem then, of course, is that if everyone can write poems then when do we find time to read them properly? It's a genuine problem and a very hard knot to unravel; my spare bedroom is piled with poetry collections of all kinds that one day I'll get round to once I've read the ones that arrived today!

MM: I love the intimacy with which you include names, like Uncle Jack, Auntie Mary, in your poems, making them as familiar to the reader as placenames you mention, eg in 'walk 1/ Top field to Bottom club, Snape Hill down past the dancing school.' How easy is it for you and the people mentioned to be named in poems?

IMcM: I think real names work. If I called Uncle Jack Uncle Jim it wouldn't seem right, even though it's almost the same word. Place names ring like bells with an authenticity I couldn't manufacture.

MM: Your humour is renowned, and you can be quite self-deprecating, e.g. in *Unselected poems 1988* you write, 'this is a booklet written by a fat bearded youth in his teens, early twenties, with certain obsessions, Dylan Thomas, horror films, Salvador Dali, comedy, folk rock, Malcolm Lowry'. In the flyleaf of *Jazz Peas*, you say, 'words are the only weapons I've got, and the only protection against the cold, and the only torches to shine in the darkness'. Can you say something about the role of humour in your poems?

IMcM: Well, I love making people laugh and I'm pretty good at it; in community arts sessions like the ones I do in Doncaster, we laugh from beginning to end just because I think that laughter makes you feel better and also it makes you feel more creative. I'm quite a serious person though: I'm constantly incandescently angry about austerity and policies that deny people their humanity and equality, and I sometimes write about that. I find it easy to do as I more or less just present a series of realistic snapshots of life round here.

MM: I'd also like to ask about the role of surrealism in your writing, such as 'Ian McMillanish thing'. Has surrealism always been part of you, or how did it start? Does it allow you to write about difficult things?

IMcM: I've always been a big fan of surrealism ever since I saw a show about Salvador Dali on TV when I was a boy; I liked what I saw as Dylan Thomas's surrealism, and I saw it as a way into a kind of dream-writing that could, as you say, contain truths that other writing couldn't approach. I also like what the poet Elizabeth Bishop calls 'the always more successful surrealism of everyday life' which is something I like to celebrate in my tweets.

MM: You're quoted as the 22nd most powerful person on radio, you're one of the best-known names in poetry – especially your presenting of the

TS Eliot readings. Can you say what poetry means to you and where it lies in the order of 'librettist, performer, writer, poet, playwright, teacher, presenter, prison and school visitor etc'?

IMcM: I think poetry is the basis of everything I do in that I'm obsessed with the magic of language and the things it can achieve, and maybe magic language is a good definition of poetry.

MM: How do you balance your time when you create, produce and perform so much: are you blessed with incredible organisational skills? I read in 'Whatever happened to Freddie Galloway' that 'Miss Parkin always knew you'd amount to something' and Mr Brown said you'd win the Nobel Prize.

IMcM: Well, I just know that if I missed a deadline or a gig they'd offer the job to somebody else. My wonderful agent Adrian Mealing has organised my life for more than twenty years, which helps. I also like to get up early, which helps. These days I'm more or less retired, which means I just do the radio work and the writing and some community artwork here and there. Mind you, as my wife says, 'retire from what?'

MM: What is ageing like for you, and what unfulfilled personal poetic dreams do you have? You write: 'I'm the ghost of somebody/ who once stood in a queue at the National Provincial Bank/ at the bottom of Snape Hill and Ian McMillan walks through me'.

IMcM: I don't mind getting old; I'm 67 now and, touch wood I'm still fit and healthy, mainly due to the amount of strolling I do. I try to do 20,000 steps a day (19,117 today so far, so I might get there); I don't always succeed, but it's good to try! I live about 600 yards from where I was born, and I feel very grounded in the place I live, and I feel comfortable growing old in it.

MM: I missed the BBC programme about father and son, featuring you and Andrew. What it's like meeting your son on similar ground? And for him? Did you always recognise his talent? Is it difficult as a parent. Do you ever collaborate?

IMcM: All my three children (I've got two girls too) were interested in what I did but Andrew always seemed to want to do something with words. I'm very proud of him and proud of the way he's ploughed his own furrow in the poetry world. We've presented a radio programme together but not collaborated on anything written; I think it might be hard for both of us.

MM: Can you explain what you enjoy about the collaboration process? You write that poetry is 'collaboration', 'a community art, not a craft pursed in a lonely room', that radio and TV are all about collaboration. In *Perfect Catch* you say you are 'a born collaborator'. Certainly, I find 'Street Girls' incredibly moving and powerful...

IMcM: I love collaborating; I like meeting other minds, other perspectives, and trying to find something we can work on together. I like writing group poems with people, and I like working with musicians and visual artists because they think differently to poets. Collaboration feels like a very human process to me; it helps us to get to places we can't get to alone.

MM: Music is clearly important to you. It shines through your language, and I learned you used to play in groups. Apart from Elvis (and REM) who were your influences? Setting aside the harmonica you found 'in your pocket', do you play instruments? I was moved by 'Fantasia on the theme of Uncle Charlie'. I get the sense of something far deeper in your poetry than you'd like to admit to? I was particularly struck by your choice on Desert Island Discs of John Cage's four minutes thirty three seconds of silence.

IMcM: I love music of all kinds; I was the drummer in a folk/rock band called Oscar the Frog and then decades later I read poems with a band called The Angel Brothers and for a few years I led the modestly-named Ian McMillan orchestra, with me speaking and musicians playing hurdy gurdy, accordion, fiddle, guitar and bass. It was fabulous to do but in the end it was too expensive to keep on the road. I wanted to have John Cage's 4' 33" when I was on Desert Island Discs because it's a piece that invites me to listen, invites us all to listen, wherever we are. I like the music of language and I love writing things with composers, finding common ground.

MM: Your love of all things Yorkshire shines through your poetry, not just the dialect, and the fact you live in the town where you were born, but noticeably around Yorkshire pudding. Have you considered a Yorkshire pamphlet or collection? So far I've found: 'The face of our Lord Jesus Christ seen in Yorkshire pudding'; 'Yorkshire pudding boat songs'; 'Yorkshire pudding boat race'; 'Minimal Yorkshire pudding'; 'Yorkshire

62

pudding rules'; 'Praise poem for Yorkshire pudding'; '101 uses for a Yorkshire pudding'...

IMcM: I don't know how many poems I've written with Yorkshire in them, but it's true that I love this place. Mind you, I guess that's to do with roots. If I was born somewhere else I'd love that place too and write about it. I sometimes get called a 'Professional Yorkshireman' which I guess is meant as an insult, but I reckon I'm un-insultable.

MM: I read somewhere poetry and sport are your two big loves – in 'The Final Score' (from *Perfect Catch*, published by Carcanet) you even coin a word 'Fubgy' to encompass football and rugby.

IMcM: Ah, I'm more of a football and cricket fan than a rugby fan.

MM: Finally, what advice might you give our readers many of whom have come to poetry following other careers?

IMcM: I would say read as many poems as you can, write something every day, and if somebody asks you to do something in the arts world always say yes because it can lead to great adventures!

Mary Mulholland

Recent publications by Ian McMillan

To Fold The Evening Star – New and Selected Poems (Carcanet)
My Sand Life, My Pebble Life (Adlard Coles)
Neither Nowt Nor Summat (Ebury Publishing)
Talking Myself Home (John Murray)

The Reading

Watch the Video

Helen Mort reads and discusses her poems
'Street Art' and 'Search Results'
which you will find overleaf.

'Street Art' was published in *Opposite: Poems, Philosophy and Coffee*, Valley Press, 2019.

'Search Results' was published as 'Search' in *The Illustrated Woman*, Chatto & Windus, 2022.

The Alchemy Spoon
YouTube Channel

https://youtu.be/2stff2DilSc

Street Art
for Daryl

You turned your son's name
into a breathing dragon, red and tangerine

and you turned the Cornbrook
tramline vista into fire,

made a man on the platform turn
into a statue, rapt in scrutiny,

the moors behind him
burning with the day's last heat.

The outline done,
you turned on your heel,

turned with the assurance
of a boy doing wheelies

on a street in Hulme,
landing every one just right, turned

back into yourself
head-down on Oxford Street

and the shadows from the bridges
wrote across you as you walked

and the city was your spray-can,
shaken, ready to be lifted.

Helen Mort

Search Results

Where do tattoos look the best on girls?
Elegant hummingbird. Mermaid with pearls.
Why do attractive women get tattoos?
99 soft feminine designs for you to choose!
Why does my girlfriend want to get inked?
Butterfly with falling leaf. Roses in wild pink.
Can tattoos look good on females?
The tip of her tongue. The blood under her nails.

Helen Mort

Reviews

Julian Bishop looks at two collections that consider gender and how to manage life in an increasingly dysfunctional world

Brenda Shaughnessy
Liquid Flesh
Bloodaxe, £14.99

Antony Mair
A Suitcase Filled With Hope
Live Canon, £10

This chunky Selected Poems charts Shaughnessy's work over two decades, from the intimate poems of 1999's *Interior with Sudden Joy* to 2019's eco-flavoured collection *The Octopus Museum* with its dystopian view of a future which uncomfortably brings to mind the present day as well. Fans of Shaughnessy's free-flowing delight in associative language and often long-form style will find plenty to get to grips with here. And she does demand close attention, her thought processes sometimes veering wildly between different themes. As she says in 'McQueen Is Dead, Long Live McQueen': 'Everything actually is blurred/ not just how you see' which could well be self-commentary.

The earlier poems feel more optimistically youthful, dare I say more cheerful than the later biting satirical poems although even here there's a sting in the tail, for example in 'Rise' where the poem ends: 'Once more, you lie with me, smelling/ of almonds, as the poisoned do.'

There's a sharp wit at work too, especially in her reflections on her own craft. In 'A Poet's Poem' she frets about using the anything-but-fresh word 'freshened' in a poem she's writing while it's snowing:

> So I went out to my little porch all covered in snow
>
> and watched the icicles drip, as I smoked
> a cigarette.
>
> Finally I reached up and broke a big, clear spike
> off the roof with my bare hand.
>
> And used it to write a word in the snow.
> I wrote the word *snow*.
>
> I can't stand myself.

So here's the great thing about Shaughnessy for me: the occasional almost violent self-mockery, the gentle humour, the music (*snow... smoke, drip... cigarette*), the immaculate line break (*as I smoked*). And also what irritates – does the poem really need the last line? Sometimes she can't resist spelling out a thought a little too literally which sometimes edges over the line into prose.

In the extremely long poem 'Is There Something I Should Know' (based on the Duran Duran song) we're told 'Sometimes I just dumped rage and hurt, yearning/ for finer feelings, not the indignities I suffered.' Parts read more like a diary although again note the masterly line break. The poem (from the 2016 *So Much Synth* collection) is part of a sequence where she uses various eighties hits to rekindle memories. Here's 'You Spin Me Round (Like A Record) – DEAD OR ALIVE':

> Words: the berries of the cosmos,
> plucked from their system,
>
> then changed beyond belief
> because you don't believe me.

It's a grand claim but her imagery more than rises to the challenge. Astronomy, bodies and (weirdly or maybe obviously) berries are recurrent.

Another long poem is the extraordinary 'Liquid Flesh' from *Our Andromeda* which considers motherhood in a very un-Liz Berry way. She describes the word "mother" as 'a kind of housecoat.. a covering like underwear' and goes on:

> Mother. Baby.
>   Chicken and egg. It's so obnoxious
>   of me: I was an egg
>   who had an egg
>   and now I'm chicken,
>   as usual scooping up
>
>   both possibilities
>   or what I used to call
>   possibilities.

Unwaveringly unsentimental, she really didn't need to worry earlier about her work not sounding fresh. And yet she covers well-trodden territory: relationships, motherhood and children although always at a slant, occasionally peppered with profanities.

My favourite section of poems is from the final collection included, 2019's *The Octopus Museum*, which surely bodes well for future work. For new readers, the book imagines a future when octopuses have taken over the world and it opens with a reflection on identity and the essentially solitary self which declares provocatively 'there is no life outside empire. All paradise is performance for people who pay.' She goes on to relate this to the queer experience: 'What could be queerer than this queer tug-lust for what already is, who already am, but other of it? […] I was a woman alone in the sea.'

Later, the poem 'Are Women People?' develops and expands the theme in a kind of Orwellian treatise on how some people are more "people-ish" than others, written in pseudo-management speak:

9.   This document seeks to discover whether women can be proven to be people.
10.   In the event that proof cannot be obtained that women are people, women will be held indefinitely (or until proof can be obtained) in a 'pre-status' category. 'Pre-status' status confers no rights of people-hood, which are deferred until the required documentation is obtained, received and validated.

Earlier in the same book she sets the scene with more satire as the octopuses consider their own status as COOs (Cephalo-Octopodal Oceanonstomy Pods) who rename themselves CEOs (Cephalopod Electro-Overlords). To sum up what I like about Shaughnessy's work: you couldn't make it up.

☙❧

Antony Mair's new collection approaches the world's various dysfunctions in a wearier although as the title suggests marginally more optimistic manner, reflected in the zingy bright colours of the cover with its sunshine-yellow suitcase. The hope, though, is suitcase-size, summed up by the gorgeous opening poem set in the unpoetic environs of an American diner:

May things always be like this: summer sunshine on the cheek,
a man's voice singing through splashes of water,
ripples of laughter in the air,
a tang of coffee against the tongue.

But strains of melancholy are never far away, an 'implacable moon' and 'irrelevant stars' lend the collection a fatalism underscored by not infrequent references to the dead. One poem is even titled 'Like Flies To Wanton Boys' where a night watching TV eating biscuits and cheese sparks a memory of a relative (?) killed at Auschwitz. This is classic Mair, although unlike Lear he's ever-aware to the possibility of a tragic outcome, the shadow 'that pulls its future behind it', a permanent presence.

Also, unlike Lear there's often redemption through love, poems that end on a smile, a pot of fresh-made jam or 'the safety of your father's arms'. The full-on joy in the poem 'You Are' (again coffee features large) is unequivocal:

You are the blue of sky and sea, of cool and of peace
radiant in morning brightness and sparkle of water;
a blue turning slowly with the earth
to the white of summer afternoons

when skin welcomes warmth like a kiss,
and fruit ripens in the market –
peaches and nectarines,
juicy and sweet in the mouth.

To counterbalance this openness, the leitmotif of a mask makes its presence felt too, reflective perhaps of a time when homosexuality was a crime, 'darkness edged with fire' as he puts it. Similarly, a boatman keeps his secrets as he ferries 'blind' tourists from a beach that is 'a barren survivor from his childhood', while in another poem the Thames runs on

…as melting glaciers
swell your waters and the seas,
drown the tennis court and garden,
make whole countries refugees.

Maybe it's because I've just been reading him, or because the world seems to be on the brink of a 1939 moment, but the ghost of Auden stalks the pages, not just in lines like the above but, for example, in the old-fashioned-sounding refrain used in 'Education':

Mummy, please tell me about global warming –
why does it happen, year after year?
There are greenhouse gases that rise, my dear;

and trap the earth's heat in the atmosphere.

The poem concludes 'it's safe and under control' which is deliberately ironic but I'd like to have seen Mair push the levers a bit harder sometimes, there's a prevalent politeness that masks (that theme again) his apparent anger.

However, subtlety is the register of this collection where poems let you in to the tick of a grandfather clock, a piece of porcelain or a soundtrack of light opera. Fittingly, the final poem with its undercurrent of mortality ends with the words '*Let go, let go*'.

Julian Bishop

Sue Wallace-Shaddad enjoys a journey with Luciana Francis which takes in childhood memories of Brazil, motherhood in the UK and questions about self

Travel Writing
Luciana Francis
Against the Grain, £6.00

This pamphlet explores what it means to be far from family and home while embracing a new life. Several poems concern motherhood. In the opening poem, 'Inventory', Francis captures a flavour of the demanding questions children can ask: 'My son asks if God was ever a baby'. A sense of wonder at the birth of a child features in 'Reminiscence': 'you were handed over like a blank page —/ our morning exhibit.' Francis goes on to describe the baby's eyes 'as new-found punctuation/ at the end of a very long sentence.'

However, the feelings of being a mother are also bound up with other relationships, such as that with her own mother. In 'The Plains',

> After missing you for years
> As I nursed, as he toddled
>
> You were in and out of the door
> Like a daily breath.

In the poem 'Lunar', the poet has a moment of recognition: 'Mother, so many memories swaddled in salt'. She looks for 'the peace that eludes me at daytime' and finds 'a brief respite from the distance. I can hear my own breathing,/ the sound of waves crashing.'

Francis explores her feeling of separateness but also recognises her new reality. In 'the distance', the poet remembers being a child, 'we were all like satellites once —/little one, how you remind me,' and she muses:

> I could stay here all night, looking upwards,
>
> on the edge of some uncharted land,
> some sort of outcast purity up for grabs,

I got a strong sense from the poems that becoming a mother has brought to the fore the poet's own beginnings and perhaps a need to re-define her new identity. 'Foreignness' is another aspect of 'distance' that runs through the pamphlet. The first poem 'Inventory' asks: 'How many more years until I belong?' and 'I am tired of being a foreigner.' In 'Lunar', the narrator compares herself to the moon, 'foreign like me'. In 'Islands', there is some comfort: 'My son will not inherit my exile'. The poem 'self-portrait as landscape' implies new beginnings where the narrator describes walking forwards

> as if on the tip of a tongue/ of a world
> open wide/ and in awe
> of itself

The poet's frequent references to time, stars, moon and sun as well as to the sea add to the feeling of a person trying to make sense of being part of something greater. She states in 'Inventory', 'Time is just another distance.' 'Cosmos' is a simple and effective poem about parenthood with the lovely lines 'Beyond the clouds,/ stars bare destinies like open palms'. In 'Time Travel', the poet begins with: 'As a writer, I can travel/ Back in time'. In my view, memory is an important component of identity and belonging.

The prose poem which ends the pamphlet, 'Home, Summer', lists personal definitions of home, such as 'fresh papaya, breeze blowing my curls'. The final example in the list is 'dancing in the streets in February, holding hands, and then letting go.' Here, the poet vividly recreates memories which may serve to anchor her sense of identity as she develops as a mother and parent. As the poet writes in 'Another Wave,' 'all we need is a touch/ to bridge the distance.'

Sue Wallace-Shaddad

Tamsin Hopkins explores three very different collections that examine racism, look at sisterhood, and take a stroll on the South Downs

Arji Manuelpillai
Improvised Explosive Device
Penned in the Margins, £9.99

Laura Scott
The Fourth Sister
Carcanet Poetry, £11.99

Claire Booker
A Pocketful of Chalk
Arachne Press, £9.99

In his first full collection, Manuelpillai explores hate crime, violence and terror. Sometimes this is perpetrated through everyday actions such as racial hate-speech experienced on the bus. Some is rooted in radical thought and may be generated by insidious and institutional racism. The poet has researched widely and interviewed former members of extremist groups. These include the author's uncle who joined the Tamil Tigers (because his parents wouldn't let him be an actor). He also interviews a member of the English Defence League who is offended by being labelled a Nazi.

Some paths are clear, their results not unexpected, but the collection allows for the multiplicity of occasions where boundaries overlap and may even be ironic: 'The neighbours next door are either having sex or arguing,/ I can't tell which, just like I can't decide where to stand/ when an anti-racist activist makes monkey noises at the EDL.'

Grief is shown often, but PTSD is everywhere in these poems, which do not shrink from the graphic depiction of violence. In 'Mortal Kombat' the speaker's nephew plays a violent video game. His immersive elation is juxtaposed with the mental cost on the game designers of producing realistic effects.

Manuelpillai uses a kind of Brechtian alienation effect to punctuate the flow of the collection, in the form of long skinny poems in which a particular truth or situation is highlighted. Each of these has a whale figure in place of a title. These images repeatedly refer the reader back to the important Melville quotation at the start of the book which discusses the sea as metaphor, and of which the following is an extract: 'Consider the universal cannibalism of the sea; all whose creatures prey upon each other, carrying on eternal war since the world began.' (Herman Melville, *Moby-Dick or The Whale* (1851)).

The poet's first whale poem draws attention to how teenagers may be deeply affected (even emotionally seeded) by racist treatment, such as stop and search policies. The third addresses the ambiguity of human existence where the need to protect the ones closest to us co-exists so closely with violence.

> most nights we tell
> our daughters
> there is something
> in our eyes
> when it is in fact
> the knowledge
> that we have
> the potential
> to do something
> they can never find out

෴

The Fourth Sister is Laura Scottt's second collection, following on from a prize-winning debut, also from Carcanet. Scott employs everyday, generally monosyllabic vocabulary and a forthright voice to convey surprising imagery and often, a left-field take on relationships, as these opening lines of 'What I should Have Said At My Father's Funeral' demonstrate: 'Let whatever it is that links me to him/ be as weak as the first skin of ice/ that grows on the squares of water in the freezer's dark drawer.'

The concepts of sisters, parenthood ('The Mother and the Son' is heartachingly, tragically lovely), boredom, memory and loss are visited and revisited in eddies of time. Birds, trees and water – especially the sea – are threaded through the collection, gathering iconic meaning as the reader progresses. The title of the book refers to Chekhov's play *The Three Sisters* and embodies the longing to exist within a trio of female friendship and love, while also testing the idea of living just on the outside of emotional ties.

The three-point structural arc given to many of the poems consists of a surprising set up, then a narrative development using unusual images and varying sentence length, and a precisely prepared ending. I think it might be this structure which makes the poems so deliciously satisfying to read. 'The Boring King' is a good example. From the opening lines 'If the past were a tree lying on its side/ and I were to go to it with a saw', we pass to the fairy-tale king of the title – 'My bleak father – the King/ of an island where trees don't grow'. The poem comes to a close:

> And as you talked on and on
>
> into the night, our sleep grew sweeter and our hair
> grew longer and thicker around us.
>
> One sunny day we woke to find you gone.

ॐ

Claire Booker's collection has the chalk of the South Downs rooted deep in its imaginative bones. The countryside, gardens and sea of the south coast populate these vigorous poems, which range across subjects as diverse as the effect on livestock of flying drones, to an elderly father remembering Easter by tasting a chocolate bunny. Booker's focus leaps between a cow imagined to be really jumping the moon, via a chalk figure carved in the hillside who dreams the sea has returned to cover the downs, to fragments of sand which are 'the condensed pandemonium of time.' Elsewhere, birds in flight are delicately rendered, and in 'The Wrasse' we are given the juxtaposition between the delicate act of hooking a fish and the brutal necessity of ending its life.

Humour and wit are employed in different forms, from the literal use of toilet humour in 'Call of Nature', to an aunt who envies luscious Italian hair, whilst her own hair is an 'under-achieving barnet/ … pumped up/ like a Norfolk turkey'. Booker also gives us the deep power of the simple and eternal. 'Mr McGregor's Seedlings' portrays a gardener who spreads love and respect of nature through his joy in gardening. In 'Footprints' a prehistoric mother makes deeper footprints when she carries her child on their journey, than when she sets him down to rest. The fossilised footprints 'walk through every mother – / a fierce, unflinching love that won't rub out.'

This collection has earned its place on my bookshelves for its wit and range of subject matter held together by a strong sense of place.

Tamsin Hopkins

SK Grout reviews three collections that examine poetry as record and resistance, how we might seek restoration from systems of power and reinvigorate our sense of selves

Chen Chen
Your Emergency Contact Has Experienced An Emergency
Bloodaxe Books, £12.99

Roy McFarlane
Living By Troubled Waters
Nine Arches Press, £10.99

Golnoosh Nour
Impure Thoughts
Verve Poetry Press, £8.50

Chen Chen's second collection *Your Emergency Contact Has Experienced An Emergency* is a bountiful collection of poems – four sections, fifty-seven poems, one hundred and fifty-eight pages. Memorably, the book is funny. This collection kept me company on public transport, at the hairdresser's and during lunch-breaks, and I never failed to laugh out loud along with Chen's jokes. A precious, rare occurrence for a collection of poems. I say precious as the collection also acts as a kind of time capsule for the years of pandemic. Not just recounting the global pressure of lockdowns, illness and death, but also the rise in anti-Asian and anti-Black hate crimes, as well as violence against queer communities, and the protests these sparked in the US (and globally) during 2020 and 2021. From 'Winter [It's April. But...]'

> I tweet about a white checkout boy who is handing a receipt to a customer, who sees me in line, who demands I step back, wait behind the red x on the supermarket floor. I thought it was my turn, apologize. Then while I'm still waiting, a white man crosses the red, steps up right behind me. The boy says nothing.

So, it is a collection of commemoration and record – but one that is uplifting and empowering, and filled with hope. It quite literally practises what it preaches. 'Instead, queer means splendiferously, you.' ('Summer [You are the....]'). The collection visibly works to negotiate with hope, while all around is despair (and death). The poems tend to have a buoyant quality whether driven by emotions, vivid descriptions or form. There is a momentum of hope within the poems – a movement back and forward, negotiating with this word. 'A student asks what to do when you're stuck. I suggest a list.' ('Winter [It's April. But...]'). The poems consider the poignancy, the delicacy of remaining hopeful too; included is a moving elegy to the victims of the Pulse Massacre: 'How does a body forget all danger, & become song, swoon?'

The collection also engages with repetition, perhaps a nod toward the repetitive pandemic sameness and the path to hope through routine. A number of poems have the same title: 'Summer' and 'Winter' pleasingly appear four times each, while 'Autumn' and 'Spring' are singular. 'Spring Summer Autumn Winter' is also included. There are eight poems with the title 'a small book of questions', each a response to Bhanu Kapil's *The Vertical Integration of Strangers* and several poems engage with school, college or spaces of learning, or use education as title: 'The School of Australia' or 'The School of Night & Hyphens'. 'Items May Have Shifted' with its dotted lines between words looks like a school exercise book. Certain words repeat across poems; my favourite was 'grackle', common to an American audience as a bird species, but of course to a poet, and a reader, additionally holds a wonderful sonorous quality. Does the bird make a grackle-like call? It certainly does across the pages.

The space back and forth between poet and reader, and speaker and reader, is one that Chen Chen often travels. Whether or not these poems are 'true' autobiographical records, they *feel* authentic, often through the use of detail, emotion and direct address. They seem to be performing the self. 'I thought this time I'd write a book / just about my father.' ('a small book of questions: chapter iv'.) Many of the poems use the poet's name or names of people in his everyday life, either in the titles or body of the poem, 'Please excuse Chen Chen from class.' ('Doctor's Note'), repeatedly refer to experiences from his life (such as a truck accident), and there is a long conversation-negotiation with his mother, despite the opening poem, 'A Favorite Room', suggesting:

> So beautiful we thought we could have perfect
> unswollen gums, be less predictable
> gay men, obsessed with our mothers.

Several poems include the use of Chinese characters, often at the crux of meaning, and another, despite the poem's long English language title, is mainly written in Chinese characters. Who are these poems for? As a reader, are we expected to decipher all of the text? Or perhaps Chen is navigating that space of language and understanding, flipping the script on mono-lingual English-speaking sections of the US, and by extension the UK. By doing so, he seems to be asking: what occurs when language is impenetrable? How do we negotiate ourselves and our sense of selves into those spaces?

> My mother has asked me to please take a look at the following, to please correct any mistakes, & please do it soon because it is due on November 1, & it is October 30. [...] I send her my completed corrections to her. She writes back: *Thanks for your help! I am always not sure when to use "the" or "on".* ['a small book of questions: number i']

This is another of Chen's forms of expression, a way of bringing language to identity, just as he does throughout the collection with the names of his friends, names of places, and his own name. The Chinese characters become an expression of his sense of self and as readers we act as conduit.

Chen asks the reader to contemplate how a poem negotiates with the page. Many of them include found language from emails, letters, lists, other poets and writers, slogans, films and songs. Indeed, some of these are letters and odes, or appear like fragments or small essays – so hybridity exists not just in language, but in form. Poems move across space on the page, in time as well as geographically – from New England, to West Texas to China.

This collection is joyous, and celebratory. It takes the reader on a journey of self-expression and of hope. Above all, it is generous. The final poem 'The School of Joy / Letter to Michelle Lin' ends with the word '*Welcome*'.

ॐ

In a recent interview with Channel 4 News, Trinidadian author Kevin Jared Hosein talked about the impetus to write his book *Hungry Ghosts*. "I wanted to give *life* to those illustrations in the history books. [...] It helps to know where we came from. It helps to know what our ancestors had to endure."[1] Roy McFarlane's third book of poetry, *Living By Troubled Waters*, bears this heavy responsibility: the need to witness, and the need to record, in order to bring life to history books. As he says in his introduction:

---

[1] https://www.channel4.com/news/could-author-kevin-jared-hoseins-new-book-be-in-for-the-booker-prize

As the poems of the present bear witness to the social issues and tragedies visited upon black bodies of the present, these incidents are rooted in a past that still hasn't been dealt with, at times when being brought to the surface draws indignation and backlash from white society. These poems cannot be read without the stories of the past being found side-by-side.

These are poems that negotiate with history; the personal history of family and forebears, as well as interrogating which events get recorded, who are the sources we trust, how do we come to terms with the past and how do we use this knowledge to seek redress and reconciliation; what does history look like as it happens around us? McFarlane generously provides the reader with an introduction, a notes section and suggestions for further reading.

In the introduction, McFarlane goes on to explain:

Erasure & Inclusion (to make known) – a term that I've devised when looking for the opposite of erasure – poems, have been created in response to researching reports and articles from the 1800 to 1850s from British and Caribbean newspapers.

The collection engages with several found texts and images; the first in the collection entitled 'Mother from her child' is an erasure poem depicting a black mother being brutally separated from her child by three white men, one who is also counting coins. Part of the text is erased, and the reader is asked to engage with the visual cruelty.

Sources of history do not just come from texts (often written by others) but from the voices of those around the poet, across time and space. 'Visitation of the Spirits' is a seven-part poem recording 'collection of stories from my mother passed down to me in the traditions of the griot' (from the Notes); these voices act as haunting, visitation, reckoning.

In many ways, McFarlane's collection resonates as both microphone and choir – giving the voices space to speak, and amplifying their stories. His opening poem is an aubade dedicated to George Floyd. Once again he negotiates the space of history – poems project the voices of members of his family, historical figures such as Yuri Kochiyama, poets such as Jean Binta Breeze and Amir Darwish, and musicians such as John Coltrane. The three-part poem 'You are Impossible to Love' appearing in each section, in the spirit of Say Their Names, records names as epigraph:

Eric Garner # Michael Brown # Tamir Rice # Breonna Taylor # George Floyd # 9 African Americans killed in Charleston during a bible study # 4 American Asians killed in Atlanta at local spas # 22 people killed in Texas # 11 Jewish Americans killed at the Tree of Life Synagogue Pittsburgh # 10 people killed whilst shopping in Buffalo, New York

I first saw McFarlane read at a pre-pandemic event, at the Poetry Cafe in London, and his stage presence and magnetic performance were unforgettable (I encourage you to seek out his live work). These poems have that rare quality of feeling like a performance at the same time as they are being read on the page. He engages a number of techniques throughout the collection: repeating names of poets (between sections and as epigraphs) such as Sonia Sanchez, Claudia Rankine, Audre Lorde; speaking with and as voices of real people, both personal and historical; enabling a kind of call & response within poems. 'Nanny of the Black Country wearing Converse All Stars' relays across left and right hand sides of the page; referencing how close those passed are still with him 'I carry her in the inside pocket of my writer's bag.' ('I must call her The Mother with the Pearl Earring'). Some poems are written in the second person, but the 'you' feels unambiguous – it's the you of history, the black bodies lost to violence through slavery or persecution as seen in 'You are Impossible to Love' Parts 1, 2 & 3.

Crossings are a major topic. From 'You are Impossible to Love': 'You are *Windrush,* the wanted in times of trouble, the visible that becomes invisible, to be discarded by a nation. You are the unwanted.' And from 'Taking Flight (I)': 'Would you not jump and watch these boats sail away?/ As you sink under, into the darkest abyss.' Indeed, the collection title is repeated several times as poem titles.

The majority of crossings recount and try to find reconstitution: 'My mother nearly drowned in the Rivers of Blood speech, she knew rivers of hate that flowed along streets, out of backyards and factories.' ('Living by Troubled Waters #1'). Poems cross time and space, as well as negotiating the historical importance of a crossing, for those moving against their will, or because they have no other choice. MacFarlane also dedicates a section of the book bringing focus to current events – 'Lampedusa', 'Rio Grande', 'Pantoum of the 27' 'for the 27 souls who lost their lives in the English Channel.' [Notes].

In some ways, there is very little room for the lyric, or impenetrability – these poems have to tell the truth, and bear that responsibility. And yet there is singing in these poems; the importance of breath in a poem, and in a body. From 'We Are A Love Supreme'

> My mother's body was a sheet of sound on a cold winter night where a travelling salesman by day and a preacher in the evenings played a tune round midnight, his hands made chords vibrate, made his own sounds in the midst of her sounds, his sax sung loud, fingers along her spine, fingers on her lips, they played through the night. A year later a child finds himself in the company of women: two mothers and a sister. A love supreme.

〆

Desire, attraction, sexuality, gender, blasphemy, madness, emotion, astrology, stormy weather and pomegranates: these words feature across the opening pages, and we are thrown immediately into the dizzying, scintillating whirlwind of *Impure Thoughts*. 'I am what they call ex tremely bi sexual', declares the first line of the first poem 'Astrological Storms'.

The collection is driven by bodily impulses, 'Wetness is my superior secret' ('The Cursed Art of Storytelling'). Nour skilfully reflects this on the page through her choice of language found in ecstasy and filth, but also in the poems' long lines, run-on sentences and verbs, and verbs, and verbs. Poems such as 'Astrological Storms' and 'Juxtaposition' call and respond to each other through their form and content.

Nour navigates a space between private, personal and public, moving the impure thoughts from the bed and/or bathroom onto the page. At every turn, she opens space for how this could make the reader feel – embarrassed, titillated, refreshed, horny? These are feelings Nour allows us to embrace, evoking an interesting play between the poems' honesty about desire and language that is usually so deeply hidden. 'I realise it is my lack of ambivalence that makes me stink.' ('Astrological Storms').

This collection aims to dance with lived encounters, authentic experiences. Many poems navigate the space between religion and desire, asking if they can co-exist. There are poems of sex and the body, but also odes and elegies, love poems, poems dedicated to injustice. 'I whisper your cities like a religious chant: Mariupol, Kharkiv, Lviv' ('Ode to

Courage') and the final poem is a moving, visceral elegy to Mahsa Amini. These poems not only live, but they consider too: 'sexuality is and isn't about genitalia' ('Cheap Tricks'). As Robin Coste Lewis once observed, 'Beauty is as old as dirt. Beauty is dark, complex, transformation—and not for the faint at heart.' [2]

SK Grout

_____

[2] https://lithub.com/robin-coste-lewis-black-joy-is-my-primary-aesthetic/

Reviews in Brief

Joe Carrick-Varty
More Sky
Carcanet, £11.99

The title poem, 'More Sky' taken from Joe Carrick-Varty's earlier pamphlet, considers the space left when a point of contact – a place, a person – is no longer there. I am sometimes disappointed to find a pamphlet reproduced in full in a subsequent collection, but in this the theme seems to have shifted from an experience of having an alcoholic father to exploring alcoholism as a form of suicide, so the pamphlet-poems seem important place-markers.

In 'All my fathers are hunting dodos in the park' the speaker, 'watching through an attic's round window' silently witnesses his father's many faces and ultimate self-destruction: 'my fathers are killing my fathers in the park'.

The poet considers some origins of alcoholism. In 'A week and not a word since the argument', the narrator's father is a child in Dublin; later 'you gather us round, whisky-whisper, *this is your Grandad,/* no liver cirrhosis, not dead at 48'. How this addiction can develop is well-captured in 'Some Dads' with the dad going from being a 'two-pint dad' to a 'twelve-pint dad' within seven lines. The implications of alcoholism for a family and the way patterns tend to repeat is exemplified in: 'this will mean/ you have inherited suicide/ the same way your body inherited/ bad knees and baldness' ('You are always the last to know things'). There is a yearning for memories to be different, such as in 'Lamech': 'the pair of us/ heading for a cinema like normal people'. These poems are well-crafted, brave, and at times painfully honest.

The second half of the book is a sequence, 'sky doc', with every poem starting 'Once upon a time when suicide was', and the line variously completed: 'another word for sorry', 'an Irish uncle', 'choosing the wrong friends', 'a room of dead dads' and so on. The repetitive nature creates a chilling inevitability.

This is a powerful, thought-provoking collection that conveys the pain and implications of an alcoholic in the family: 'maybe/ we had come to finish our fathers/ maybe to finish ourselves'. Notably the book is dedicated to 'the stayers', with the narrator expressing his determination not to follow his father's path, for it is not a given: 'Sometimes I Talk to Myself as if I'm on a Chat Show': 'he isn't coming back dad ffs we have three options/ here but let me tell you the fourth option/ STOP WALKING TOWARDS THE SEA I will not/'.

Sarala Estruch
After All We Have Travelled
Nine Arches Press, £10.99

Many of the poems of Sarala Estruch's debut pamphlet are also in this, her first collection, with the bulk of them in the final (fourth) section. I read this as an intention to explore the backstory of her Indian heritage, the discovery of which was the overriding theme in *Say*.

Her parents' love story seems to offer the poet inspiration. In 'To leap', she writes: 'I want/ to write about learning to live// with doubt, learning to rise in it/ learning to love like that'. This allies with a second theme of the book, the role of motherhood. In 'Return' there is a sense of pride in the mixed races her own children carry, the speaker having also formed a relationship with someone from a different race: ' 'The children are *very* mixed' I grin./ 'They are universal,'.'

Several images recur, for example, severing and cutting: in 'Kesh (I)' and 'Kesh (II)', this seems to illustrate transgenerational patterns. In '(I)' the young man who was to become the poet's father rejects Punjabi tradition by cutting his hair: he 'brings the blade back and forth, back and forth, witnesses the severance'. In '(II)' the narrator chops her hair off on the eve of visiting her blood grandparents in India: 'time to be shorn of the past'.

Another repeated image is red and green. In 'The Measure of Water' the speaker is warned 'not to dress in red or green'; in '[Portrait of a Rose]' '/ red disaster   on a stalk/ of deep green thorns'. The rose seems a vital image. In 'I research the origins of the modern rose & discover', the rose 'becomes what she is'.

Form-wise, Estruch includes pantoum, several column poems, which can be read both ways and possibly reflect the poet's mixed inheritance, and the collection ends with her evocative 'Ghazal: Say'. Shortly before this is the inventive poem 'Camera Lucida', written in twelve text boxes over eight pages, including two blank pages (entitled '[following several empty pages]') set out a bit like a photograph album. In 'IX – [Camera Lucida]', the rose image resurfaces: '*I am looking at* [a rose through the] *eyes* [of my father]// – the closest I have been to him in decades'.

Just as the modern rose, symbol of love, travelled from the East and exists alongside the English rose, so too these poems cross time and continents. In 'Arand Karaj', there is a sense of resolution as the narrator imagines meeting who she might have otherwise been, 'that alternate self, born of a union/blessed'. These are lyrical poems of love and loss, evocatively presenting a coming-to-terms with an inheritance.

Safiya Kamaria Kinshasa
Cane, Corn & Gully
Out-Spoken Press, £11.99

In this debut collection, Safiya Kamaria Kinshasa, British-born of Barbadian descent, combines her skills as dancer, poet and choreographer to reclaim ancestral voices. Much visited tourist destination, Barbados has less to boast about its past as a leader in the slave trade. This book reads like a prayer to black enslaved African-Barbadian women, acknowledging the abuse they suffered and its effect upon subsequent generations. These women left no written record, but their gestures were recorded by white Barbadians. By analysing these texts through labanotation[1] Kinshasa recreated their movements, then danced them in order to create these poems.

Illustrations of these movements intersperse the poems in a visually affecting way, even if a little hard to understand. Similarly, many poems are written in dialect which made reading slightly challenging. However, read aloud, the pain, powerlessness and musicality of their voices could be heard:

<blockquote>

do you know wat
it means tuh pull a country from yah chest tru yah neck?
walk widdout a home believin
you is a good fuh nuttin girl?

</blockquote>

('12 Shots Who Warned Me 'Sweet' Was Dangerous')

The details in the creation of this book silently call our attention, for example the preface only appears one-fifth of the way in, as if depicting an unacknowledged past. Kinshasa says in 'Preface: And If by Some Miracle': 'I discovered the enslaved were speaking, constantly.// One woman shook her head while gagged with iron, another made circles with her arms in the cane field'.

Some lines particularly stayed with me, such as: 'never give your child an inheritance it cannot use' ('Sometimes Death Is a Child Who

---

[1] a method of recording bodily movement (as in dance) on a staff by means of symbols (as of direction) that can be aligned with musical accompaniment.

Plays With Rubber Bands'), succinctly conveying the complications of holding a legacy of opposing sides.

Many poems carry an epigram, such as *St Michael 1824* or *St John 1688*. These represent districts in Barbados and I assume the dates refer to texts studied but may hold deeper significance[2].

Kinshasa is confident in her experimentation. For example in 'Gully' syllables are separated by commas, creating breathlessness, or trauma: 'an, ud, dur, gul,ly, his, his, his, his, bit, de,/right, side, ah, my, neck, my, knuc, kles, lob, bied, ag, ain,'

Some poems are harrowing to read, such as 'i doan wan massa wassssste me/   if i were   a tree   i'd   feel no whip', ('Avoid Direct Contact with the Skull)', but there are lighter moments, as in 'Across-Atlantic Child':

> i once watched de whole Nativity
> > three wise men passed each other
> > de police came

> > de police stayed longer than de donkey
> i lied   i didn't watch it all

This book rewards careful reading. Each time I return to it, I find more.

Charlotte Baldwin
With My Lips Pressed to the Ear of the Earth
Nine Pens, £7.50

In the title poem, the speaker is addressing her mother (presumably mother Earth): 'I am sorrier/ than any child who ever learned, too/ late, what it means to be ungrateful.' This title is close to the Apocrypha, Sirach 21:5: '*The prayer of the poor goes from their lips to the ears of God, and His judgment comes speedily.*' However in Charlotte Baldwin's poem, 'There is no reply.'

Baldwin has a distinctive, lyrical voice and lightness of touch as she explores the disasters facing earth. In the surreal 'I shit a white rabbit' the narrator is in an Airbnb and has to decide what to do: her choice between 'me, the rabbit, the flush handle'. How tempting to leave the 'mess' she created and drive home as if nothing had happened.

---

[2] For example 1688 was also the year 'The Act for the Governing of Negroes' was passed

Baldwin never spells out our individual responsibility. She is far more subtle, she's off sharing 'an ale with John Barleycorn' or sitting 'in a circle in a park because nature is very healing' ('Eco-Therapy'); she becomes 'The Wolf-Bride' because 'better a wolf than a man for a husband [...] who 'knows the joy/ of loping beneath snow laden trees'; she's busy writing 'Guidelines for Walking Your Pet Snake Safely', making eyeshadow out of mothwings, sending an 'RSVP to Robin Goodfellow', and finding the Bronte sisters at Pizza Express, where they leave 'poems about birds/ on the silver dish in place of a tip'.

'The people are thirsty' the poet writes in 'The Woman in the Well' as if to explain man's attitude to depleting the world's resources; in 'Keeping My Bones Just So', she writes, 'to be human is to be hungry/ all your life'.

Baldwin has a wide range of tone, from mythic 'You greyed my young hair and sold it/ to the grasshoppers for their bowstrings' ('Letter to a long-term illness'), to carrying a sense of urgency, as the reader travels with a bullet down a gunbarrel 'towards a pair of mild brown eyes with a red light marking their midpoint' ('Meat Dream'). The reader may laugh uncomfortably at 'The Obligations of Confessional Poetry' when Baldwin writes 'Confessional poets use 'I's the way some cooks use salt'.

The pamphlet ends with 'Bright Carver', after *Gormenghast*:

cut cut cut for the dryad
cut cut cut for the dragon's head
big trees tight with futures
we hush their whispering

Peake's work is 'full of splendour and darkness, but also has gentleness, humour, pathos, beauty, tragedy and a love of the written word'.[3] I found this true too of Baldwin's pamphlet; it has a rhythm and mythic quality all its own.

[3] https://www.theguardian.com/books/booksblog/2014/aug/16/gormenghast-masterpiece-mervyn-peake

Tim Tim Cheng
Tapping at Glass
Verve Poetry Press, £7.99

Tim Tim Cheng's pamphlet starts quirkily in a bathtub (*'soap! soap! soap!'*) then takes the reader on a journey that draws upon the poet's experience of being born and growing up in Hong Kong and her subsequent relocation to Scotland.

Readers will encounter the Goddess of the Moon, 'speechless crags', paddy fields, a back tattooed with a 'flaccid penis', porn discovered on a father's tablet; there are poems about the speaker's father and granny, many references to freedom and a need to escape. Her poems are also concerned with language, identity and home. In 'Waterlogged', she writes about moving from Hong Kong to Edinburgh:

> If I were to make this place
>
> my home, this language I've lived
> outside but scratched at,
> would the news back home get old?

There is a feeling here of being on the outside looking in, as suggested by the glass (transparent yet a barrier) of the title. It also suggested to me the fairytale Cinderella, which is referenced in 'Kindergarten'; breaking, an image that recurs (for example, in 'Shockproof' which opens: 'There are so many ways of breaking'); and fragility – and there appears to be a faltering romantic relationship; in 'clouds and clouds', she writes: 'the air is not warring/ but we are'.

I found the title phrase in 'News Nocturnal', in the closing line of the first stanza, 'the sound of someone tapping at glass'. This poem also refers to Raja Shehadeh, the Palestinian human rights lawyer who writes on environmental issues, democracy and freedom, themes close to Cheng's heart. His 'book calls me from my old shelf./ I read it at work. I read it before sleep/ to the shouts of protests,'. Perhaps the idea of glass also alludes to political transparency, for example in 'Salt and Rice', she says: *'You can't eat democracy like rice,'*.

Cheng's poems are playful and cover a lot of ground, though at times left me disorientated and unsure what was going on. I felt this was the intention, to reflect the speaker's own sense of dislocation.

Kerry Darbishire
Jardiniere
Hedgehog Press, £10.99

It came as no surprise to learn Kerry Darbishire is also a songwriter, for these lyrical poems comprising her third collection have a pronounced musicality.

Darbishire blends narrative with detailed observations of the natural world and location, particularly in poems set in Cumbria where she has spent her life. She has a talent for stilling time, such as in the opening poem, 'The House of Lost Land' when she writes 'Outside a door to birth and death asleep/ in lath and lime', and 'the signature// of a hand pressed into the north wall/ where we can't help but place our own.' The 'we' brought the dedication to mind, '*for Barbara/ our times together*', and the collection reads like an elegy, for a loved one, for a way of life. In 'The Seekers', the narrator sits in a church to 'peer/ unnoticed through rows of Sunday caps and hats/ and mourning black'.

Many are poems of gratitude and wistfulness, such as 'Seventh Spring': 'I give thanks for wounds/ their grace   their strength/   to heal'.

The book is divided into seasons. Summer introduces music (Elvis, the Beatles) together with holiday jobs, trips to Greece and Andalucia, reminding the reader the ordering is also charting a life: 'Today is your birthday,/ the first time we cannot be together' ('Birthday').

Darbishire's images are often filmic, such as the dressed salmon 'set in the centre of the table like an open coffin' ('The Salmon') and she regularly awakens other senses too. In 'December Morning' 'a night sky/ spiced with all the Christmases I remember:' and 'Outside the mid-winter orchestra:'; in the title poem 'the smell of drenched earth in our hair'.

'To Autumn' has a lovely repeated line: 'Nothing has died/ just absent', and there are poems to 'The Windermere Children' and Jacqueline du Pre, '*the golden girl*/ in her bluebell-blue silk dress, playing as if she had invented music' ('Falling Silent'). The poet writes movingly about her parents 'my mother's bruised skies/ my father's bed of leaves' ('The House that Grew in me'). The penultimate poem, 'Returning' evokes that sense of timelessness that coexists in time: 'I felt nothing had changed/ evening air holding the scent of pine/ sycamore and ash taking the weight of rain'.

This is an evocative, sensitive collection of poems that offers time to reflect, and evidences the healing power of the natural world.

Julian Bishop
We Saw It All Happen
Fly on the Wall Press, £9.99

This is without doubt a book for our time. Bishop, with his background in television journalism and deep-rooted interest in the natural world, blends an investigative eye, sensitivity, irony and admirable technical skill: golden shovel, villanelle, sonnets, lipogram, acrostic, palindrome to name only some. Razor-sharp humour helps the reader see how we are all implicit in climate catastrophe, while his playfulness with language extends to regular double meanings.

The collection itself is arranged as three-course meal, with 'A Taster', 'Mains' and 'Afters', offering more sinister implications of environmental disaster, whether it's mussels cooked by an overheated ocean, hippos unable to wallow, salmon unable to spawn... And these are simply among the starters.

The title poem similarly starts ordinarily enough, a family watching a David Attenborough documentary: 'the new *One Planet/* though it started ages ago   catching it all/ on repeat'. The narrator holds the TV zapper (echoing the electronic insect-killing machine):

> tucking into a Deliveroo
>   got the zapper in my hands   channel trawling
>   prawn toast   popcorn calamari
>   they're going down well

Bishop uses rhyme to witty effect: 'We need another Amazon' appears in two columns that can be read either way:

> eyes bowed down   *in a tropical trance*
> somewhere distant   *gardua bamboos dance*
>
> then a voice in the distance   *somewhere in the blue*
> cries *mind the gap*   *the word is falling through*

The poet's use of imagery is accomplished and vivid: the mammoth is a 'thick-skinned galumper', and titles entertaining, such as 'Hope is a thing with Tubers', 'I'm Hooked On The Jellyfish Live Cam' and 'Welcome to Hotel Extinction'.

Reading the collection, it felt increasingly fast-paced and unrelenting, as if Bishop is paralleling the acceleration of environmental damage. We are the accuser and the accused. Yet he holds onto optimism – just. In 'Ash', the closing poem, the bleakness of the current state of the world is conveyed by 'My heart has darkening rings about it' and 'it's hard to see stars in the dark'. Nevertheless, the poet ends with hope that Nature will survive: 'I imagine a tangle of branches extending a cage/ around Earth, like fish in a coral cave. Forests would follow, in a mass revolution/ of leaves, a green solution to pollution.' This, Bishop says, is 'A last desperate gasp to save the planet'. If people read and heed this book, his dream may take root.

Maria-Sophia Christodoulou
A Disbelief of Flesh
Out-Spoken Press, £8

British-born Maria-Sophia Christodoulou explores her Cypriot roots in her debut pamphlet. I read this as a book about grieving, not just for the dead, but for the past that lives on in us under the skin. Part personal journey of discovery, part exploration of heritage, culture, faith, the pamphlet is dedicated to the poet's late Yiayia (grandmother).

The opening poem, entitled 'End', has the extraordinary last line, 'We call on the Holy Mother to forgive the dead for dying.' At first I read this as a stage in the anger process, then saw it more as a desire to engage with life, the way each generation sheds the past, though echoes remain. 'We are all someone's somebody else' the poet writes, 'scrunched with sounds we only hear in the dark.'

The grandmother is remembered in several poems: she would 'soothe our cuts/ with soaked koulari' ('Somewhere in the Hiatus'); in 'Grief/ing' 'In church,/ there are so many of her–/ clutching her dust-leather handbag [...] Her blazer pinned with a bead-eyed/ insect brooch'.

The curious title appears in the closing poem, 'Plum Girl': 'I empurple my body/clouds of skin hidden/ in a disbelief of flesh'. The bruised colour perhaps signifies the pain of rejected aspects of self, while 'every part of me ripens/ when accepted.'

Christodoulou has a pared-back style and is adept at creating filmic images, such as when her grandmother 'grips the village like roots of trees/ surrounded by icons of women/ in glory, saint men standing –' ('The Last Woman in the Village'). There are several religious references. In 'Unfaithful Altars' 'God is pouring wine/ over the tablecloth, writing/ *to be mundane is a sin* in the wine'. But the speaker writes 'Forget praying./ We have alive' ('Happy Place'), and in 'New Home Ritual' she seems to embrace new or ancient ways: 'In darkness, we bless this house,/ burning sage, sighing into our pillows'.

This is an evocative slim pamphlet epitomising grief in honouring the past, endeavouring to lay it to rest, and finding new ways of being. In 'A Lesson in Moving On': 'but if I can, I will be better/ in another self, another self and another,/ until the world runs out of people'.

Mary Mulholland

Contributors

Ruth Aylett teaches and researches computing in Edinburgh and has been known to perform with a robot. Her poetry is widely published in magazines and anthologies, and her pamphlets *Pretty in Pink* (4Word) and *Queen of Infinite Space* (Maytree) were published in 2021.

Dickon Bevington is a poet working in children's mental health in the NHS and charity sector for the past three decades. Three years ago, he moved onto a rusty old narrowboat on East Anglia's River Great Ouse.

Alison Binney is a poet and English teacher from Cambridge. Her debut pamphlet, *Other Women's Kitchens*, won the 2020 Mslexia Pamphlet Competition and was published by Seren Books in September 2021.

Julian Bishop's first collection of eco-poems, called, *We Saw It All Happen* is published by Fly on the Wall Press (2023). A former environment reporter for the BBC, he is a former runner-up in the Gingko Prize for Eco Poetry.

Carole Bromley is a York-based poet. Three collections with Smith/Doorstop and one with Valley Press. Winner of a number of prizes, including the Bridport and the Hamish Canham Award as well as the 2022 Caterpillar Prize for poems for children.

Roger Camp lives in Seal Beach, CA where he tends his orchids, walks the pier, plays blues piano and spends afternoons with his pal, Harry, over drinks at Saint & 2nd. His work has appeared in *American Journal of Poetry, North American Review, Gulf Coast, Southern Poetry Review* and *Nimrod.*

Lorraine Carey's poems have appeared in *Poetry Ireland Review, Abridged, One, Panoply, The Stony Thursday Book, Atrium, The High Window, Ink, Sweat and Tears, Orbis, Prole, The Honest Ulsterman, Foxglove, Poetry Birmingham* and *One Hand Clapping* among many others. She has work forthcoming in *Magma, Softblow* and *The Cormorant.*

Rachel Carney is a creative writing tutor and PhD student based in Cardiff. She won the Pre-Raphaelite Society Poetry Competition and was voted runner up in the Bangor Poetry Competition in 2021. Her debut collection *Octopus Mind* will be published by Seren Books in July 2023.

Deb Catesby has been writing poems for the past two years, taking a series of courses with the Poetry School and with Arvon. She is also a painter, working from her studio on the Hereford/Worcester borders. Previously she wrote plays and taught Creative Writing to degree level to mature students.

Oliver Comins lives and works in West London, but his poems have been published quite widely and collected by Mandeville Press and Templar Poetry.

Claudia Court began writing in earnest on her retirement. She has had work published in a variety of journals and won several competitions. Her debut collection, *How to Punctuate a Silence,* was published in 2020 and her second book, *School Milk,* in 2022, both by Dempsey & Windle.

Patrick Deeley is from Loughrea, County Galway. His poems have appeared widely, and seven collections were published by Dedalus Press. His awards include the WOW2 Award, The Dermot Healy Poetry Prize, and The Lawrence O'Shaughnessy Award.

Michelle Diaz has been published by *Poetry Wales, Under the Radar, Lighthouse Journal* and numerous other poetry publications. Her debut pamphlet *The Dancing Boy* was published by Against the Grain Poetry Press in 2019. She is currently working on her first collection.

Eileen Farrelly's poems have appeared in *Marble, Anti-Heroine Chic* and in anthologies. Her chapbook, *Some things I ought to throw away,* was published in 2021. She is also a songwriter, she can be found singing in pubs around her hometown, Glasgow.

Viv Fogel's new collection *Imperfect Beginnings*, Fly on the Wall Press, February 2023, explores what we're born into, what's passed on, and how we make meaning from it. Previous collection: *Without Question*, 2006 and pamphlets *Witness*, and *How It is*. A psychotherapist, she lives in London with her partner.

Mark Fiddes has recently been published in the *Forward Book of Poetry, Magma, The Moth, The North, Poetry Review, the Irish Times* and *The Brixton Review of Books* among others. His latest collection *Other Saints Are Available* was published by Live Canon.

Deborah Finding is a queer feminist writer. Her publications include *fourteen poems, The Friday Poem* and several anthologies. She won the Write By the Sea 2022 Poetry Competition and was commended in the Troubadour International Poetry Prize 2022. Her debut pamphlet is out with Nine Pens in June. www.deborahfinding.com

Rebecca Gethin has written six poetry publications. She was a Hawthornden Fellow and a Poetry School tutor. Her next pamphlet will be published by Maytree Press later in 2023 She blogs sporadically at www.rebeccagethin.wordpress.com

Kristel Gibson moved all over the American West. A former film photographer, she now uses her best camera: whichever one she has with her. She lives in Seattle with her husband and their dog. https://www.flickr.com/photos/kwyo/

SK Grout (she/they) is an editor and writer who grew up in Aotearoa New Zealand, lived in Germany, and now splits her time between London and Auckland Tamaki Makaurau. Her debut chapbook is *What love would smell like* (V.Press, 2021). https://skgroutpoetry.wixsite.com/poetry

Alex Harford enjoys photography, art and writing (in all sorts of genres), visiting places that don't seem real, the outdoors, reading (mostly flash and fantasy short stories), films, and music. https://AlexHarford.uk

Sarah Hemings is a Poet and Chartered Librarian from Bristol. She has twice won First Prize in the Gloucestershire Writers' Network Poetry Competition. In 2021 she was mentored by Fiona Benson. Her debut pamphlet, *Night after Night in the Quiet House*, was published by Maytree Press in October 2022.

Georgia Hilton is an Irish poet and fiction writer living in Winchester, England. She started publishing poetry relatively late, after having her three children. Georgia is the author of two books of poetry, both published by Dempsey and Windle, as well as a collaborative pamphlet published by Nine Pens Press.

Tamsin Hopkins writes poetry and fiction. She has an MA in Creative Writing from Royal Holloway, London and is a previous winner of The Aesthetica Prize. Poems have appeared in *Mslexia, The London Magazine, Magma,* and *The Alchemy Spoon.* Her pamphlet *Inside the Smile* is published by Cinnamon Press.

Jane Hughes is a psychotherapist in private practice in the north of England. At the age of 58 she is proud to be a student, studying for a PhD in creative writing.

Kit Ingram is a Canadian poet and writer based in London. His poetry has appeared in *Ambit, Magma* and *The North.* Last year he was longlisted for the National Poetry Competition. *Aqueous Red*, his debut UK collection, is forthcoming from Broken Sleep Books in 2023.

Trust 'Tru' Katsande is a freelance photographer based in Ontario, Canada. He specializes in street, event, portrait, and philosophical art photography, capturing moments that tell a unique story. Trust also enjoys exploring cinematography and script writing. Trust owns a fashion business that he takes great pride in promoting. https://alphatribeclothing.ca/

Ian Ledward is an artist and writer living in Scotland. An active member of the Open University Poets' Society and Fife Writes, his work has been published in several national and international magazines and anthologies including *The Heimat Review, Bindweed Magazine, The Sonder Literary Journal, Dreich* and two Giffordtown Writers Anthologies.

Millie Light is an emerging poet from West Cornwall and has recently been published in *Full House, Ink, Sweat and Tears, Shooter, Spelt, Mamecology, The High Window, Intersections (NI)* and a few anthologies. She is a PhD researcher at Ulster University, Belfast.

Michael Lyle is the author of the poetry chapbook, *The Everywhere of Light* (Plan B Press) and is an ordained minister. His poems have appeared widely, including *Atlanta Review, The Carolina Quarterly, Crannóg, The Hollins Critic, Plainsongs* and *Poetry East.*

Ian McMillan is a writer and broadcaster who presents **The Verb** on BBC Radio 3. He's currently writing a Yorkshire version of *The Barber of Seville* for Bradford Opera Festival. Ian watches Darfield Cricket Club. The only time he played cricket, at Low Valley Juniors in 1963, Mrs Hudson told him to take his balaclava off or she'd make him wear his mother's Rainmate.

Sarah Mnatzaganian is an Anglo-Armenian poet based in Ely. Her debut, *Lemonade in the Armenian Quarter*, won the 2022 Saboteur Award. Poems have appeared or are forthcoming in *The Rialto, Poetry Wales, The North, Magma, Poetry News, Poetry Ireland Review, PN Review, The Frogmore Papers, Poetry Salzburg,* and *The Alchemy Spoon.*

Helen Mort is a poet, fiction and non-fiction writer from Sheffield. Her collections *Division Street, No Map Could Show Them* and *The Illustrated Woman* are published by Chatto & Windus. She's a Fellow of the Royal Society of Literature and teaches creative writing at Manchester Metropolitan University.

Emma Ormond is a writer from Cambridge, England. Trained as an entomologist, the natural world features heavily in her work both in its actual and fantastical forms. She began writing again in her late thirties, most recently her poem 'Heritage' received a special mention in the 2021 Bournemouth Writing Prize.

Robyn Perros is a South African writer and PhD scholar. Her work has been exhibited/published in spaces such as the KwaZulu Natal Society of the Arts, Symposium for Artistic Research in Analog Photography, Institutions & Death Conference, *Nature is Louder, Isele, Decolonial Passage, Mahala, Zigzag, Ons Klyntji.* robynperros.tumblr.com @robynperros

Colin Pink's poems have appeared in a wide range of literary magazines. He has published two pamphlets *The Ventriloquist Dummy's Lament* and *Wreck of the Jeanne Gougy* and two full-length collections *Acrobats of Sound* and *Typicity*. He posts a six-line poem every day on Instagram @colinpinkpoet

Rob Primhak is a Sheffield paediatrician and medical educator with a BA in English Literature. His medical writings have been published in the UK, Europe and the US, and his poetry has appeared in *Poetry Wivenhoe*, and an anthology, *But Not Defeated.*

Jim Ross jumped into creative pursuits in 2015 after a rewarding research career. With a graduate degree from Howard University, in seven years he's published nonfiction, fiction, poetry, photography, hybrid, and plays in nearly 200 journals on five continents. Photo publications include *Burningword*, *Feral*, *Litro*, *Kestrel*, *Phoebe*, S*tonecoast*, *Sweet*, T*ypehouse*, and *Whitefish*.

Anna Saunders ('a poet who surely can do anything' - *The North*) is the author of *Communion*, (Wild Conversations Press), *Struck* (Pindrop Press) *Kissing the She Bear* (Wild Conversations Press), *Burne Jones and the Fox, Ghosting for Beginners, Feverfew* and *The Prohibition of Touch* (all Indigo Dreams).

Mark Saunders lives on the Isle of Wight. His poetry can be found in *Abridged, The Cannon's Mouth, Confluence, The Interpreter's House, Meniscus, The Museum of Americana, Red Ogre, Soft Star, Spelt* and *Strix*. He has appeared at Ventnor Fringe Festival and other venues.

Donald Sellitti is retired after a thirty-eight-year career in research and teaching at a medical school. He has published extensively in medical journals, and has recently had poems published *in Autumn Sky, Better than Starbucks*, and *Rat's Ass Review*, who nominated his work for a Pushcart Prize.

Di Slaney runs Manor Farm Charitable Trust and Candlestick Press. She was the winner of The Plough Poetry Prize 2022. Her poems have been on BBC Radio 4, widely published and highly commended in the Forward and Bridport Prizes. Her collections are *Reward for Winter* and *Herd Queen* (Valley Press).

Thea Smiley is a Suffolk poet. Her work has been shortlisted for the Bridport Prize and the Live Canon Collection competition 2022, commended in The Hippocrates Prize, longlisted in the Rialto Nature and Place competition, and published in magazines including *The Alchemy Spoon, Spelt*, and *Ink Sweat and Tears*.

Sue Spiers lives in Hampshire. Her poems have appeared widely in print and on-line including *Acumen, The North* and *Ink, Sweat and Tears*. Sue works with the Winchester Poetry Festival, spoken word group Winchester Muse and edits the annual anthology of the Open University Poetry Society. Sue tweets @spiropoetry.

Jill Vance is a poet and interdisciplinary artist. Her poems have appeared in *Truth Serum Press, Pure Slush, Dirigible Balloon, Sipping Cocoa* and *Green Ink Poetry*. She hopes one day to have a pamphlet published of poetry and artwork.

Sue Wallace-Shaddad has an MA in Poetry from Newcastle University. Clayhanger Press will publish her latest book, a collaboration with Sula Rubens R.W.S., *Sleeping Under Clouds* in April 2023. Dempsey & Windle published her pamphlet *A City Waking Up* (2020). Sue is Secretary of Suffolk Poetry Society.
https://suewallaceshaddad.wordpress.com

Rod Whitworth, born in Ashton-under-Lyne in 1943, has done a number of jobs including teaching maths (for 33 years) and conducting traffic censuses (the job that kept him on the streets). He now lives in the Garden City (aka Oldham) and is still tyrannised by commas.

Veronica Zundel has had poems published in *Magma, Snakeskin, Ekphrastic Review* and several anthologies and has won the Barnet and Cruse Lines prizes. Her poetry has featured on BBC Radio 2 and in an Open University foundation course. She has an MA in Writing Poetry from the Poetry School/Newcastle University.

Illustrations

Page 3   *Don't let poetry die*, Seattle. Photographed by Kristel Gibson, 8 September, 2007.

Page 8   Strawberry Field, Liverpool. Photographed by Viv Fogel, 2019.

Page 12   *Surrender Dorothy* 1986, Washington D.C. Photographer unknown.   https://www.washingtonpost.com/local/surrender-dorothy-painted-on-a-beltway-overpass--whats-the-story/2011/06/23/AGduf6kH_story.html

Page 16   *Got Ya*, Derelict School Building, Newcastle-under-Lyme. Photographed by Alex Harford, 2014.

Page 23   Parkland Walk Tunnel, London. Photographed by Viv Fogel, 2016.

Page 31   14 Rue Froissart, Paris. Photographed by Mary Mulholland, 20 February 2023.

Page 38   *Outside the Headmaster's Office*, Derelict School Building, Newcastle-under-Lyme. Photographed by Alex Harford, 2014.

Page 47   Homebase Store, Newcastle-under-Lyme. Photographed by Roger Bloor, March 2023.

Page 52   Graffiti briefly seen on a building in Montreal. Photographed by Jim Ross, August 2019.

Page 67   *Oi*, Derelict School Building, Newcastle-under-Lyme. Photographed by Alex Harford, 2014.

Page 102   Harare, Zimbabe. Photographed by Trust 'Tru' Katsande, 2018.

The Alchemy Spoon Pamphlet Competition

The winner will receive a publishing contract with Clayhanger Press, 25 free printed copies of the pamphlet and an online Zoom book launch.

Rules for the competition

Opens 1 August 2023
Closing date: 31 October 2023

The prize pamphlet will contain 24 to 32 pages of poetry.

Entries for the competition should be 8 to 10 poems that showcase the poet's work. The winner will be invited to submit up to 32 pages of poetry for their pamphlet.

All poems must be entirely the entrant's own work. Individual poems in an entry may have been published online, in journals or magazines, or multi-author anthologies, provided the writer retains copyright.
You may submit up to two entries, each of 8–10 poems, provided an entry fee is paid for each.
Results will be emailed by 31 January 2024 to all who entered, and published on *The Alchemy Spoon* website shortly afterwards.
The entry fee will be £10 each or £15 for 2.
Entries must be paid for, and your entry file uploaded, by the closing time of 11.59 pm on 31 October 2023.

Full details of the competition and the link to enter your submission can be found on *The Alchemy Spoon* website and on Duotrope.

Submission Guidelines

We welcome submissions of up to three brilliant, unpublished, original poems on the issue's theme through the website during the submission window. You will find full details of how to submit on our website: www.alchemyspoon.org.

We are only able to accept submissions from those over 18.

If you have poems published in the current issue of *The Alchemy Spoon*, then we ask that you wait out one issue before submitting more work.

Simultaneous submissions are permitted but please tell us straightaway if a poem is accepted for publication elsewhere.

We aim for a speedy turn-round and will respond to every submission, but we don't offer individual feedback.

Authors retain all rights. However, if a poem is then published elsewhere, please acknowledge that it first appeared in *The Alchemy Spoon*.

Our submission window for Issue 10 will be open 1 – 31 May, 2023, the theme for the issue will be 'Friends' and we will welcome poems on this theme up to 40 lines. See our website for the full details.

Submission Guidelines for Essays
If you have an essay on some cutting-edge poetry-related topic, please send it to us during the submission window for consideration +/- 1500 words.

Submission Guidelines for Artwork
We are always looking for original artwork to feature on future magazine covers. Portrait-orientated images work best (or images suitable for cropping). Good quality lower resolution images can be sent at the submission stage, but higher res files will be needed (2480 pixels x 3508 pixels) at print stage. Please email us with your images as an attachment.

Submission Guidelines for Reviews
If you would like to recommend a poetry collection or submit a review of a collection, then please email us or use the contact form on the website.

Poetry Workshops
The Alchemy Spoon editors offer a one-to-one poetry feedback and workshopping service without prejudice via Zoom or Facetime. All profits from this contribute to the cost of running Clayhanger Press. Please email requests for feedback to: vanessa.tas@btinternet.com to arrange this.

Cover Design by Clayhanger Press

Typesetting and Design Roger Bloor
Senior Copy Editor Sara Levy
Proof-reader Adam Lampert

www.clayhangerpress.co.uk

Clayhanger Press

Printed in Great Britain
by Amazon

20910038R00061